CREATIVE IDEAS FOR CATECHISTS

Bringing Children's Faith to Life

Ruth Ann Rost

Sheed & Ward™ is a service the The National Catholic Reporter Publishing Company.

ISBN:1-55612-987-4

Published by: Sheed & Ward
            115 E. Armour Blvd.
            P.O. Box 419492
            Kansas City, MO 64141-6492

To order, call: (800) 333-7373
www.natcath.com/sheedward

To my husband, Charlie, and our nine children.

To the pastor, Rev. Richard Sirianni,
the staff, and the faith-community,
especially the children,
of St. Mary Magdalene Parish,
Portland, Oregon.

To my colleagues in Religious Education
throughout the Archdiocese of Portland, Oregon.

INTRODUCTION

This book is an extending of the hand and heart of a fellow children's catechist; one who thoroughly enjoys helping them to discover, experience and own the Truths of our faith through creative catechetics. Together, we are called to be children's catechists. Unto us they come to be touched with the gifts which we have received. They come to taste of the mystery to which their inheritance of faith is calling them. Is there a higher call than to be for them someone who helps to make their believing a living reality? someone who breathes love upon their tender faith? someone who offers holy light in which their budding belief can flourish? Our catechist call is a gift to be cherished, yet given again, and in the giving there is but more blessing extended.

Indeed, we who are called to be a children's catechist can expect to be thrice-blessed! First, we are blessed in our own receptivity to the Gospel message and its evermore fruitful application to our lives. Second, we are blessed in our helping children to open their lives in experiencing the Good News also. Our third blessing lies in our willingness to exercise our gift of creativity within our vocation as a religious educator. And, as is often the way of blessings bestowed, these have a way of compounding even more into our, and our children's, lives. Such is the way of the Spirit at work, ever increasing the yield in our good ground.

As a children's catechist for over twenty-five years, I have often been witness to this mystery of continual blessing. Whether in the primary religious education classroom, in programs of sacramental preparation, or in celebrations of the liturgical seasons in our large family, the promised blessings have flowed both into and out of our efforts in ministry. Our God, who delights in creating life and blessing it, is evermore generous toward catechists. Our receptive stance, then, is just to be ready with open hands and hearts. These pages are offered to help that openness and its joy to happen for you in creative catechetics.

We begin in Chapter One with the pleasure found in acknowledging and exercising our own innate gift of creativity as an intended sign of our faith-full living and wholeness. It is this profound gift which we are encouraged to employ in calling forth and enriching children's faith-journey; its activity is meant to be a gratifying and joyous experience.

Chapter Two emphasizes the faith-fullness of the catechist, and challenges us with several necessary hallmarks of our discipleship. It also offers helpful suggestions for prayer-moments which support our faith-fullness.

Well before students enter their gathering space, the creative catechist, aware of its impact upon them, prepares for its positive influence. Chapter Three presents suggestions for enlivening the room in preparation for their rich experience of faith learning and development while on their holy ground.

As we get to know our children, and meet them on their most natural ground for learning – namely, their five senses – we will help them open to faith truths through environment and activity which promotes their participation and receptivity. Chapter Four guides the creative catechist in the technique of sense-it-ivity in faith education: those stimulants to learning and many sensory "vehicles for the truth to ride on."

Chapter Five outlines the catechist's ultimate aim of offering a lesson in which children come to own some Truth and relate it to their lives. A great lesson's result depends upon several critical factors in preparation, presentation and procedure which can be successfully coordinated, always with the empowerment of the child as the catechist's primary concern.

Because as a children's catechist we are committed to helping them experience oneness with God in their prayer, we feel that this subject, so foundational to our ministry, needs consideration in this context of creative catechetics. Chapter Six furthers our understanding of children at prayer, and offers scores of practical ideas for primary- and middle-graders' full involvement in "making prayer." Here, too, the catechist is aided by suggestions to further develop and enrich the experience of prayer. Various styles for both adults and children are outlined to encourage growth in prayer experiences.

Chapter Seven explores the boundless treasury of all types of resources which can be employed in creative catechetics. Since their incorporation into our faith environment and lessons directly affects the responsiveness and participation desired, these indispensable learning-tools are essential to our planning and realization of great lessons. Discussed here, too, are the many resources essential to our own spiritual formation, a work which, as we show throughout the book, must go hand-in-hand with that of unfolding a vibrant faith-life in children.

May this book serve you well as you employ and enjoy its suggestions for experiencing fresh dimensions of faith-living. May these ideas support and strengthen your ministry of bringing children's faith to life. Let us join our creative hands and hearts together in these blessing-times.

An artist
is not some special kind
of human being;
every human being
is a special kind
of artist

John Ruskin

CHAPTER 1

ENJOYING OUR GIFT OF CREATIVITY

"Creativity"

Planting a garden, sewing a blouse, painting a chair, designing a poster, dancing a jig, framing a picture, frosting a cake, hooking a rug, painting a sunset, digging a hole . . .

"Creativity"

Whistling a refrain, expressing an opinion, praying a petition, decorating a church, cleaning an attic, ministering to the aged. . .

"Creativity "

Folding a napkin, surprising a child, praising in wonder, offering an excuse, preparing for emergencies, making a sandwich, making a wish . . .

"Creativity "

Heading a family, telling a joke, pastoring a church, lifting a burden, greeting the day, filming a celebration, cleaning a garage, earning a living . . .

"Creativity"

That blessed profundity with which we move through life, making each step, and each footprint, so personally *ours*. From toddler days into elderhood, we are caught up in creativity's magnetism. Its charm lures us. Its compulsion satisfies. Its expression fulfills. Its drive propels us into the glorious experience we name *life*.

"Creativity"

Ever a mystery to be pondered, embraced and celebrated!

"Creativity"

What on earth is it? Do I have it? How can I use it? How might I truly enjoy it?

"Creativity"

What a wondrous concept to think about! What a marvelous idea to dwell on! to explore! Such is our gift of *creativity*. In considering the connotations of the gift, we may well find ourselves with the dilemma which St. Augustine felt when he was asked to give the meaning of time. Said he, "If you don't ask me, I know what it is, but if you do ask, I simply can't tell you." Just so might we puzzle over the meaning of this wondrous gift of creativity which has influenced humankind since its birth. It is right and good that we, as catechists, ponder and truly marvel at creativity's power and its possibilities and that we appropriate its dynamics in our lives and ministry.

A simple definition may help us here. *Creativity is the unique expression of an idea.* It is the free revelation of what is felt, thought, learned and perceived. Tailoring the definition to a personal fit, we can simply say, "My creativity is my unique expression of my idea, of what I feel, think, know, etc." My creativity shows you *who I am!*

THE GIFT AS SIGN OF THE GIVER

How precious is our creativity! How sacred it is! Through our creativity we show one another how uniquely we are responding to the life which we all share. Using this inner power, we reveal what is happening within ourselves. Some truth about ourselves is, then, shared. Our individual creative expression becomes our fingerprint, indeed, our soulprint on the world, for no one experiences life exactly as another does. No two people interpret experiences exactly alike. What a treasured gift given to explore and develop! Through our creative expression, whether we are age 5 or 95, we come alive in the highest sense. Our delight deepens as we allow our creativity to reveal the very presence of our Creator within us. Our joy takes root, and grows, as we manifest the very glory of God in ourselves fully alive!

This concept of ourselves as creative beings—of having the ability to express ideas—deserves further probing if we would understand our gift well. Ponder for a moment who comes to mind when you think of "a creative person"? Walt Disney? Michelangelo? A degreed architect? American frontier pioneers? A child building with blocks? Surely, each of these and, indeed, every human being should be included therein. How is this so – that every child of God possesses innately the power to express one's unique and invaluable creativity?

The answer is given in the first chapter of the Book of Genesis: we are created by a creating God. If we define our Creator as supremely self–expressive, what idea is, then, being revealed throughout creation? What might God be showing us ? Surely, and most profoundly, God is continually revealing *love*. And God, the divine Creator, is forever expressing the desire to *give life,* to be united with every created thing out of this expressed love. Because God's creative expression continues on every level of life, each particle of creation expresses God's love. Each of us, then, is an idea of God's love, and will be revealed so forever.

Further, each of us is created "in God's image." We are meant to be *like* God, from whom we have come. Thus, each of us has inherited creativity. It's already within us! Creativity is in our very human nature, freely implanted within each person. This Truth should excite every human being made by God's hand, for as we allow the divine 'spark' in our being to reveal our unique ideas, our thoughts and sacred individuality, we are joyously impelled to express ourselves creatively. The creative glory of God, then, returns to God as we open up to the divine gift within. Our own health and well-being flourish, as we respond to this impulsion to wholeness. Life itself is celebrated with enthusiasm, as we find satisfaction and fulfillment in our creativity. Thus, our spirit enjoys the creative energy for which it was conceived, and in which, by divine intent, it has no bounds.

"UNLESS YOU BECOME LIKE LITTLE CHILDREN"

How we delight in watching little children employ their gift of creativity! How naturally they "make something." They seem lost in thought as blocks become a castle, brush strokes become a zoo and a box of old 'dress up' clothes become a whole new world of personae. We watch, and sometimes wonder what their secret might be, that such abandon could be so fulfilling and such experiences could be so rewarding. How fortunate for us that, if we would be willing to let the little child teach us, we, too, can discover – really, re-discover – our own amazing gift of creativity. For as a certain small poster delightfully prompts our grown-up sophistication to observe:

"I AM A LITTLE CHILD
I PAINT FEARLESSLY
I HAMMER LOUDLY
I BUILD RECKLESSLY
I WRITE ORIGINALLY
I SING RAPTUROUSLY
MAY NO ONE QUELL MY CREATIVITY
ONLY REFINE IT"

If we have already uncovered one of the secrets to child-like enjoyment of our creativity – that is, acknowledging that the gift is already there – then the next logical step lies in seeing ourselves in the 'refining' process of our gift. This simply means that as adults, we clarify, cultivate and own our gift in a deeply personal way. Not for its perfection, which often renders it lifeless. Not for an ulterior gain exclusively. But, as with the child, to experience self-expression for its own sake: simple enjoyment.

Perhaps, for many of us, a simple, child-sized step in returning to our appreciation of the creativity within is all we might need to once again enjoy its power. In setting aside our intimidations and self-imposed limitations, we can find ourselves freely following the impulse to its divine, illimitable potential. Out of who we are becoming (which seems more clear to ourselves as we move through more of our life experiences) we can, in joyful abandon, reveal our individual response to those insights, learnings and perceptions which have become so uniquely our own. Emphatically, it remains for us to allow the inner vision of our creativity to "come alive"!

One day many men were working on the excavation of a city block. Rubble was being hauled away. Heavy equipment carved the exposed earth. Fresh foundation was laid. The old building would give way to the new. When asked what it was they were doing, one workman answered, "I'm cleaning up a big mess." Another replied, "I'm making a living." A third responded, "I'm building a great cathedral." One of the workers had allowed the vision of his activity to come to life with the sense of his creativity.

RELEASING THE POWER OF OUR INNER VISION

The more we allow our inner vision of ourselves as creative persons to be accentuated in our lives, the more intensely will its power be released and enjoyed. As the little poster suggests, *"only refine it."* And we who are called to be a dynamic teacher of faith will generously grant the overflow of our gift into the lives of our children as their creative catechist.

Happily, most folks do, in many and varied ways, envision life creatively. Although perhaps not always consciously, each of us is continually expressing our individuality. We make many creative statements every day. Our gift might have a musical voice, or an artistic flair. It might make a literary statement, or have a dramatic bent. Our selection of clothing, our style of home-decorating and the countless expressions of our personal tastes all speak about ourselves with creative assertions.

At times, our gift might be at work quite deeply hidden, as we employ it in arriving at keen insights to the mysteries around and within us. Quite conclusively, our creativity serves our internal living by opening us to the revelation of our godliness so that, using our spirit eyes, we see the Divine at work in our world. How valuably creativity serves our continual conversion, by revealing our inner being in all its uniqueness, to ourselves and to others. Presumably, our gift of creativity is meant to flow both *into our lives* and *out of our living* in order for it to accomplish its divine and holy intention.

WHAT IS CREATIVITY'S "WORK" IN OURSELVES?

As Christians, we believe it is in God's plan for our humanity to reach its fullness, wholeness and potential integration, beginning in this earthly life. We will be complete as persons when we are fully alive in body, mind and spirit. It is into this fullness which we are led with our gift of creativity. How vital to our well-being is our cooperation toward reaching our life's fullness and our integrity. How glorifying to our Creator is our appropriating this gift.

So, we might rightly ask ourselves, when and how am I most alive, most aroused to reach my personal potential to wholeness? What is it that makes the difference between being "half asleep" and being fully, integratedly alive? We turn to our Creator for answers, since it is to the extent that we *receive* into our being the revelations God has given to us, and to the degree that we *perceive* God's presence in the natural world (in designs, patterns, textures, fragrances, colors, sounds, etc.,) as well as to the measure that we *believe* in the power of the Resurrection dwelling within ourselves – to these degrees can we each call ourselves fully and integratedly alive! To these extents we can call ourselves people who are indeed "putting on the mind of Christ." Creativity's task, then, is to open us to harmonious, responsive living, toward consciously realizing (bringing to reality,) our divine potential. For nothing less than such full living unfolds for the man or woman who responds to such a divine plan as revealed in Christ. How purposeful, then, becomes our existence when we realize that the more alive we are the more we have to give to each other. Living becomes giving. By creative living, and through more fully integrated personalities, we become more complete as a person. It is this very manner of generous living which celebrates the divine life within us.

How fruitful it is to be continually impressed that, as God's children, our most natural way of living is *creatively and expressively.* Jesus Christ, in his triumphant rising, has restored and made available to us all the power and fullness of our original humanity. It remains imperative for us to appropriate the grace continually offered to us: grace which uplifts our innate creative powers unto their original potential. Quite simply, it remains for us to live vitally and as redeemed people should!

I believe that God intends for us to reveal our unique creativity for, ultimately, the greater good of others, too. Each of us has a portion of the other's completion, of the other's well-being. As obstacles which tend to prevent and inhibit our creative expression are gradually overcome, we are more free to be oriented toward others' good, as well as our own.

LETTING THE CHILD WITHIN LEAD US

It is good, then, for us to wonder, "What can I do to live more creatively?" Let us explore some possibilities.

First, we need to renew our child-like sense of being alive. We need to fall in love again with *life* itself, life all around us, life within us. Take some time to really watch a freespirited child, and let one teach you the sheer *wonder* of being alive. Everything is exciting. Everything needs exploring, discovering. Life is to be lived *now*! No moment must be wasted; there is so much to touch, taste, smell, see and hear! Through the senses the whole world becomes thrilling, real, inviting and worthy of attention. We need, then, to return to the wonder and mystery of sensing the life all around us, really being "sense"-ative to all that living is offering us. Opening up our senses to the beautiful natural and human life all around will re-awaken our responsiveness to our precious gift of life itself – indeed, our first generous gift from our Creator.

This return to a childlike inner freedom can invigorate our manner and very outlook toward others. Enjoying our gifts of wonder and imagination, we become a more spontaneous, optimistic person. Joy and enthusiasm characterize us, when perhaps boredom and disinterest had prevailed. We are newly enabled to slough off layers of unhealthy seriousness in our approach to living, the more we learn to embrace experiences with the openness and "Wow" of a child. Furthermore, as we grow in childlike self-abandonment to the God of love, and thus, relate more simply and comfortably to our Creator, there develops within us more of a true and genuine worship. As this freedom rings within us, our creativity is so easily brought into play. Our very living begins to make creative statements. We find that we are happily more able to see life as God desires His children to perceive it. And it is, of course, found to be *very good!*

LETTING OUR INTERESTS TAKE THE LEAD

We have considered that our creativity begins to come to life when we let two things happen: (1) when we sense our experiences with the heart of a child and (2) when we perceive natural life and our interior living as wonder-filled. These insights open us to an integral relationship with our God. Too, they lead us toward the natural, personal creative interest which correlates to our uniqueness. We seem increasingly drawn, then, to this wholeness of living, and the more we are inclined to it, the more life-giving its completeness becomes for us.

So, let the joy and fun of our gifts begin! Let the divine urge for full integration be rewarded in our search for those particular creative activities which give genuine pleasure. Skip on down the path of those interests, perceptions, pursuits and pastimes which, with inevitable practice and skill, can lead to so much satisfaction. Part of each day should find us not only "making do," but, indeed, "making" and "doing"! The refinement of our creativity beckons and, surely, the Spirit is ever at work as our guide.

Such a wide variety of creative activities are available today that one's happy dilemma might well be in which selection to pursue. Some consideration of resources, including craft and hobby outlets, one's particular state in life, as well as those very individual interests and inclinations will surely lead in making decisions.

Decline not to use someone else's idea, pattern or direction, to foster your creativity; yet, it is ultimately our personal and unique interpretation of them which matters to our wholeness and satisfaction. Why is this so? Simply, I am more interesting when I express my individual conception when my soulprint, as we have seen, is on the activity. And the world is, thereby, more interesting with my unique contribution added to the life we all share. The creativity of each of us becomes like a pulse with which our common life throbs, as we bless each other with the gift of our fullest selves.

So, enjoy discovering your interests! Enjoy being open to your creative bent! Will it be gardening, dancing, quilting, hiking, writing, poetry, gourmet cooking, puppetry, making music, making soup, painting a picture, painting a room? Pursue your "thing." *Do your thing!* Return often to that creativity which interests you, which recreates you in the finest, truest sense. Participate regularly in that venture which renews, integrates and nourishes you. Simply, for the pure joy of it, do that creative activity which expresses *you!*

SATISFACTION GUARANTEED OR TRY AGAIN

Throughout my own adult life, creativity has definitely played center-stage roles in helping to maintain a sense of wholeness and health. Its dynamics have long affected my commitment to our marriage and a family of nine children, particularly as we developed cherished family customs and traditions which remain indelibly impressed and continually observed, along with the variety of celebrations of the Lord in our home throughout the liturgical year. Involvement in parish life, too, has included using our gifts of creative expression shared in educational settings.

In living the faith in our home, it is often the intense, sensory involvement within our liturgical celebrations which please and teach all of us so much. The lighting of the home-made Christcandle so ceremoniously at the Easter morning table, the decorating of the home altar in Mary's honor, hanging colorful symbols on an Advent Jesse tree, the setting and resetting of the little figures in the Nativity crèche – all of these expressions help to make the celebrations ours. All have been, and continue to be, our own soul expressions, indeed.

In reflecting a bit, I believe it has been in "finding myself" through creative adventures which has satisfied so fully. Various modes of self-expression have found (and "saved") me, too, throughout the busy years, since some forms of creativity always seemed inviting when release and renewal were needed. Veritably, in and out of interests I have drifted happily in many a season. And new, exciting ones continue to lure temptingly. I fondly recall my tole-painting and découpage era. Cross-stitching, sewing, flower gardening all have been balm to this oft-frenzied spirit. My brief, but so prolific, stint of herbal gardening came to an abrupt halt last summer when the mint plants threatened to take over the entire plot. But, what fun those good digs were! And then there was the afternoon when I wound a pile of grapevines into 23 chubby wreaths. Ah, the memories linger on, even as I make plans to embroider someday soon a favorite saying, *"Living well is the best revenge"* whenever time allows.

Homemaking has often been one extended creative expression. Rooms are made cozy with our collecting and crafting. Handmade quilts have warmed us. Hand-finished furniture has rested us. Knitting has clothed. Poem-writing and journaling have delighted. Doll-making has refreshed. As our home reflects us, it becomes sacred space where, in our creating, we are created ever anew. *Indeed*, "I will persevere in the way of integrity within my house," as Psalm 101 proclaims for us.

THE NATURAL FLOW INTO CREATIVE CATECHETICS

As the substance of this book will attest, creativity has become a vital part of my catechist call over the years. What delight is a classroom with bright colors expressing the Truths of our faith! Walls and prayer centers become veritable cups running over with inspiration possibilities. What power and joy are released in both catechist and children when self-expression is allowed its full range of movement. Such becomes the blessing we give to one another. There may be no other dynamic which reaches as far into our experience of pleasure as does creative expression in matters of faith. Rightly included, passive creativity, too, such as listening to soothing music, praisewalking on a spring day, and "picturing" a story being told, all serve our inner need for balance, focus, recreation and rest. The creative catechist, as we shall acclaim, will surely discover growing satisfaction in ministry upon releasing the power in one's blessed gift of creativity.

SHARING IN DIVINE UNLIMITEDNESS

I believe it is crucial to our capacity for enjoying our gift of creativity that we remain open to the unlimitedness of our potential. To set down stifling margins and boundaries to our capabilities is most assuredly to cripple and eventually to deaden the full enjoyment of them. The gift, freely given and meant to lead us into fullest life, is like a seed, in that it is planted for becoming fruit as its natural development occurs. In fruit there is no end, for within it is but another seed. And so with ourselves. And, as surely as "life begets more life," our freed-up creative energies beget more of the gift. Growth occurs. All kinds of development become possible: emotional, mental, spiritual and social enrichment, to name but a few potentialities. When our uniqueness surfaces, we shine more brightly with the light of our individuality for having done or created something, having perceived the Divine or experienced an event, which only we could have accomplished. Is not this how life is meant to be celebrated at every age? Let the creative catechist, foremost, affirm such ideals strongly, that one's creative gifts might flourish more fruitfully with every opportunity!

We have seen that involvement with creativity enlarges our sense of integration and wholeness. It helps us feel connected to power greater than our own. We feel fruitful from our efforts. Most importantly, the harmony we experience energizes us to demand more from our very living; it pushes us on in the quest for improvement of skills, for healthy achievement. It stretches the perceived limits of our capabilities. This, truly, is God at work within our humanity, for our God is all about *more life*. How our God loves the word "more"! Indeed, let us never limit the Giver, nor the gifts offered within creativity.

One of my favorite contemporary musicians is a young man named Tony Melendez. This talented song writer and guitarist can move one to tears with such songs as "You Are His Miracle." Hearers seemingly can't get enough of the heart and soul which Tony pours so creatively into each of his renditions. Gifted, he simply gives. He allows the song to personally express him. And being in his audience, one can see even more of Tony's uniqueness and creative unlimitedness. For Tony Melendez literally has *no arms*. He has learned to express his musical ability with his *toes*! Truly, as his song reminds us, "we each *are* His miracle waiting to be."

The more each of us allows ourselves to live creatively, the more our spirit, and our spiritual sensitivity (our intuition, perception, and receptivity) will grow to healthy fulfillment and maturity. We will "see that which is hidden to the eye," see the Trinity in the symbol of the three-pronged stigma in the crocus center, see Eternity in the infinite circle of a lowly onion ring, we will wonder and awe at a spider's lacy web, know Christ as we break bread at a meal together. With our spiritual senses, a bouquet of flowers or a bowl of soup can become a prayer. Our life-visioning will become as an interior hologram, leading us beyond mere limited realities. And it will come to "see and touch Christ" in those to whom we minister and serve.

The above exciting Truth struck me quite emphatically, and somewhat humorously, at a time when I was helping an elderly neighbor. She had acquired a stubborn infection on her foot, and after several weeks of careful, daily attention to it, we both began to feel somewhat discouraged with its very slow healing. No change seemed apparent. On one of those days, I had prayed on my way to her home, "Lord, I'll do this, but I'd really like to feel that it's not just this troubled woman I'm helping. I'd like to see You when I help her with this tedious infection." On that day, while the offending foot soaked in its warm bowl, we visited about her youthful days spent in another city. "You know," she offered conversationally, "I used to have some very good Jewish friends." Startled, and with a secret smile, I reacted with renewed spiritual sensitivity, thinking, "All right, Lord. I hear You. And thank You."

CREATIVITY: EXPOWERMENT FOR THE JOURNEY

In a true and deep sense, living creatively is a way of loving oneself as we are commanded to do. When our physical senses are in harmony with our Creator's intent, and when we are willing to stretch our innate abilities of envisioning and perceiving, we are contributing magnanimously to our own healthful living. So it is that whenever we move through the day with the heart and soul of our inner child, we come so much closer to that dimension of life which we call divine. And whenever we take time to refresh our whole person by expressing our particular interests creatively, we add to the delight of our own life, as well as to others' who share in it.

This is as it should be, surely! Let us affirm such empowerment with the open-armed enthusiasm of the six-year-old youngster who exclaimed, when seeing the Pacific Ocean for the first time, "Oh, wow! I wanna go in the *deep* end!" It is not for us to paddle about reluctantly at the shore's edge of creativity, unwilling to discover where its gift will carry us. We're made for the deep end!

Life, for us who are called to bring forward the faith of children, must not be a passive and uninteresting existence. No, we are called to acknowledge and embrace God's gift of our creativity in its broadest sense of experiencing all of life as praiseworthy, in its profound, intuitive sense of perceiving its fullness beyond the momentary reality, and in its applicable sense of "making and doing" that which uniquely expresses our personality. For it is through, and with, and in creativity that we are led on our journeying into our fullest experience of life. The tag on the gift says, *"open and enjoy."*

Modern man listens more willingly
to witnesses
than to teachers
and if he does listen to teachers
it is because
they are witnesses.

Pope Paul VI
Evangelii Nuntiandi (No. 41)

2

BECOMING A FAITH-FULL CATECHIST

Having considered two vital qualities within ourselves as children of God, namely, our gift of creativity and our impulsion toward full living as creative people, we turn our attention toward ourselves as a children's catechist. This particular ministry in the Church seems to ask a response which is born of a deep desire to "let the children come to Me." We are the Peters, Jameses and Johns, the Marys, Marthas and Peggys, whom the Master calls to assist the little ones in their faith. Responding to this summons, we allow our gift of faith to be touched, called forth and shared. Our name is "salt," "yeast," "light" within the circle of children. Gifted, we want to gift in turn; called, we call forth. Our commission as a catechist is highly esteemed in the Church's ministry of building up the Body of Christ, for we hold the hands and hearts of the very Kingdom of God in our midst. Jesus pointed to our children who exemplified the faith He would honor. Our acknowledgment as their catechist challenges us to be all that our children need and deserve in their formation in faith.

It is imperative to our charge that we allow our own faith and spiritual living to be developed as fully as possible. This consent will help shape us as a more receptive channel for the flow of the Living Water of Truth in and through ourselves. This faith development as necessary, is essentially the work of one's being well-grounded in the Truths as taught by Jesus and His Church. It means being well-rooted in the Good News through study, reading and the use of developmental resources. We allow our spirit, thereby, to be formed and conformed to the Spirit of Christ Risen, and our very living, through Sacrament, community-orientation and service, to be filled with Christ's life. The catechist needs to be eager for faith to develop indeed, for it to be ever a 'work in progress,' for one's effective catechesis is dependent upon one's faith-full and full commitment to the Church's Truths, and to the living out of the Gospel with an uncompromising attitude toward it. Nothing less ought to be our self-expectation when we answer "yes" to our entrustment! Such willingness for faith development promotes the "good ground" for the Word within to grow and produce its ultimate fruit.

Thankfully, opportunities for faith-enrichment and spiritual growth are available today in a wide variety of forms. The learner might select readings from the classic or current spiritual writers. One might attend a day or evening of reflection. Studying Scripture with a group, participating in a parish renewal or other adult education programs can also be occasions for recharging one's spirit and commitment.

Consulting one's local diocesan newspaper for places of area workshops, retreats and conferences might further promote faith-building. Perhaps a group of fellow catechists would enjoy such an event, with such an experience multiplying enthusiasm all around. Attending an in-service day especially for catechists will surely reap the fruit of learning about applicable topics which often enlarge, too, upon the theme of the current Catechetical Year. Such gatherings bring together one's fellow catechists, who often enrich one another through prayer, shared ideas and renewed dedication. Whatever the formation opportunities at hand, take advantage of as many as possible! See them as ideal ways to satisfy the hunger and thirst for growth, vital signs of the catechist responding wholeheartedly to one's call.

THE CATECHIST'S DAILY PRAYER

Critical to the formation of the heart and mind of the Christian catechist is one's daily prayer, the time of being present to and communing with the living Lord. The habit of making a special time for dialogue and holy silence is vital to one's conformation to Christ. What, then, might be some components of one's prayer-time which will lead to more fruitful and faith-full living? Let us consider a few:

1. *Detaching.* 'Emptying' the mind, heart, emotions being needy before God, relaxing physically, being in a peaceful setting, perhaps Nature's gifts will help, lighting a prayer candle, hearing soft music, lowering lights can aid detachment, too.

2. *Inner focusing.* Realizing God's presence surrounding and within oneself, being fully loved, valued, forgiven, heard, understood, gifted with endless life, accepting all such dispositions from a loving and personal God and Savior.

3. *Releasing oneself to God.* Surrendering to God's love, resting in God's loving care, being totally heart-to -hear together, letting God sustain oneself in His love, presence, power and promises. This depth might be nonverbal, with eyes closed serenely; there might be prayer gestures: bowing, open hands, arms raised. Sometimes one has tears, sometimes spontaneous song, praying in tongues. "Imagination with God" is freeing, as is inner dialogue with God. The Spirit gives us prayer-gifts to use, enjoy, assist. These mentioned draw one deeply into the sense of there being only God in these moments, toward being open to God's revealing love.

4. *Renewing in God.* Desiring one's further inner conversion, seeing oneself living and believing more in the persons of the Trinity, firming-up one's resolve to BE as God would have one: living-out the gifts and fruits of the Holy Spirit, renewing one's willingness to change and 'break' from what separates one from fruitful living in God. Often one's deep

prayer might close with a concrete resolution, expressing readiness to activate renewed faith, hope and love. Above all, a fresh commitment to the will and plan of God seems to pervade the heart from such moments spent in prayer. (See Chapter 4 on Helping Children Experience Prayer for further suggestions on prayer for the catechist.)

Reading the liturgical scripture selections for the day, meditating on their messages with 'long thoughts,' and writing one's reflections in a notebook (creating a simple prayer journal) can all be helpful components of daily prayer. One's creativity might extend to entitling the journal with a particular "piece of scripture" and letting this theme flow throughout the current liturgical season. How deeply personal becomes the reflection/writing time of our daily prayer, then! Attending daily mass, with its supreme gift of the Eucharist, of course, assists faith formation profoundly. The catechist who makes time for daily prayer, and who strives to faith-fully abide in the Lord throughout the day, can rely on the communion and inspiration which will surely flow from the Spirit in abundance.

PLEASE, DO PASS THE 'SALT'

If it's true that there is strength in numbers, it is surely and emphatically so for two or more catechists who gather in God's name for a few moments of prayer before classtime. In the Lord's presence we are both energized and able to be one another's support in ministry. Encouragement in our mutual commitment bears its fruit from these prayer moments later when we are with the children. Simply, through prayer our needs are met. It's a *promise*!

PRAYER LEADS INTO A DEEPER KNOWING

Prayer, then, like the continuous current of a fresh stream, carries us along in an ever-deepening knowledge of Christ and His Spirit. He, Who continually unfolds all mystery for us, leads each heart into deeper knowledge of Himself and of God's will. Thus, we are gracefully inspired to:

Know who we are – that we are "Ephesians 1 and 2" people chosen, bestowed upon, called for love, predestined, adopted, redeemed in Christ, and made wise for understanding the mystery of Christ. In Christ we *know whose we are* a people covenanted to God, who belong to God through our rebirth at Baptism the ensealed of the Holy Spirit who alone has formed us in God's image. We are God's, yes, we are God's. And out of this profound Truth, we come to *know where we are!* We are in the vineyard of the Church, as workers for the harvest of all that Christ has redeemed; we are on a journey to life forever in the Triune God. We are "in the world, but not of it," we are on our way to our true *home*.

Essential? Fundamental? Indispensable? Prayer, for the catechist growing ever more deeply in Christian transformation, is, most assuredly, all of the above.

A prayerful reading of Ephesians 1 and 2 illuminates our profound identity in Christ. The faith-full catechist, concerned with developing this identity, will continually seek the discipline of prayer and opportunities for enrichment which will promote such closeness, the fruit of which will then be apparent in our discipleship; namely, in our bringing children deeper into *their* faith identity. For in our ministry will be discovered four particular hallmarks which will distinguish us as a faith-full catechist: *conviction, commitment compassion* and *conversion*. Let us consider carefully these valid indicators of our faith-fullness.

CONVICTION

Today's catechist must, primarily, have a passionate *conviction* of the very *need* for children to learn the Truths of Jesus Christ and His Church; to learn and, thereby, to base their very lives upon them. It is so very critical to this fulfillment that our learners derive meaning from Jesus' coming, living, dying, rising and remaining *with* and *for* us! Such conviction will compel us to provide catechesis and faith experiences for children to know about God, but further, to know of God (as in the Biblical sense of 'knowing,' which is encountering). By our faith-full modeling, and continual affirming of our own relationship with God-in-Christ, our youngsters will be led to build up their budding faith, and to develop its meaning for and application to their everyday lives.

Gradually they, too, will come to accept responsibility for the building up of Christ's kingdom. No greater desire should stir within the catechist's heart than our children coming to this unwavering and active belief in their indwelling Lord. *This* is faith education as it must be! So much more than the intellect must be touched. Knowledge *alone* is not power. Knowledge is only *potential power*! With encountering numerous personalities to 'believe in,' today's naive, spiritually unformed child can readily line up Jesus along with one's favorite television or sports heroes as ideals of Truth incarnate. Early and consistently, the child's spiritual gifts of Understanding and Knowledge must be refined, so that one might build up steadfast faith in and grow in union with Jesus Christ alone. Let us be unwaveringly convinced that only the Truth must be fed to our 'lambs.' By virtue of their Baptism, it is the food they are entitled to receive for nourishment.

To support our affirming of the importance of superlative catechesis, we must also be convinced that our special contribution to this mission, by the use of our unique gifts, truly matters. "Feed My lambs" commands us to use all that we are and have, so that ours might be well nourished and truly revitalized at every stage of their spiritual growth. My 'piece' of the Bread of Truth must be extended to every child who, quite often, doesn't even realize he/she is hungry for it. So, be deeply convinced of your vital contribution, prepare for it carefully, sit in prayer with its Truth yourself, and trust in its effect upon its receivers. Indeed, the faith-full catechist will teach best only what he or she has first deeply known.

So it is that our convictions about embracing and presenting the Truth will shape our faith teaching. Indeed, our convictions will ultimately help to shape the desired faith response and convictions of our students. Surely, our dedication must always be to this end.

COMMITMENT

Also contributing critically to our formation as faith-full catechists is our personal commitment to the whole Truth of the Good News of Christ, full commitment to the Truth, from Creation to the cross and resurrection, to the apostolic commission as sharers of the message and mission. Our children will witness our witness to the Truth that there is an expectation attached to our Baptism; that is, that we are called to be life-givers to others. No one is 'exempt' from this commission to lay down our lives, to fearlessly cooperate with the Holy Spirit in our dying to self, that there might, therein, be *new life* in Christ.

As our children encounter (and are affected by) this commitment to life within us, they shall see, hear and encounter *true life*. They will begin to believe in, and *experience* their own true and full life. How vital is our personal commitment, then, to the whole Truth? It has been well said that "the witness must first of all *be* something for Christ before he or she *does something* for Christ." Our commitment to the Truth must, then, be a deep and unwavering *being* for Christ in every area of our lives. Out of the well of this primary commitment we will be able to draw up the promised Living Water which alone will satisfy the spiritual thirst of our children. Let our commitment overflow, thus, into their lives. As faith teachers committed to high standards of lesson presentations, we find ourselves continually searching for ways to enrich and enlighten these precious moments, so that young lives might, ultimately, bear their fruit. How might the following three key considerations contribute to high catechetical ideals and the goals within this commitment?

(1)   Careful and thoughtful lesson planning
(2)   Greater understanding of children's intellectual and spiritual needs
(3)   Seeking catechetical enrichment toward growth in proficiency and spirituality

Let us first enlarge upon our commitment to careful planning.

Thoughtful Planning Rewards Catechist and Children

Planning our presentations for children's faith learning is best begun when we sit with our lesson in prayer to let its Truths first touch our faith, to let the Spirit enable us to give that which we have, thereby, received. In moments of receptive and open-hearted prayer, more of the Truth is welcomed in, owned and synthesized within ourselves, the first movements necessary before imparting it to others.

Our preparation will begin, too, with awareness of the impact of the learning environment that 'space' where children enter in, gather together, see, hear and experience Truth and learning, where they will meet love, acceptance and respect, where they can give relaxed attention in an orderly and secure setting. More of these vital aspects of preparation will be outlined in a further chapter which discusses them more fully. Indeed, how profound is the impact of the faith learning environment!

Thoughtful planning must also include our sensitivity to our children's various learning styles and needs, in order to direct the Truth and its accompanying expressions in ways which will most effectively meet their needs. Therefore, we will check various resources to assist us in choosing ways and means for providing for maximum impact upon our learners. Committed to helping all the students, we will necessarily meet them on the ground of the learning ability of each child to the very best of our capability.

Systematic evaluation following each lesson will further sharpen our awareness of strengths and weaknesses in presenting, and will ultimately improve both teaching and learning. Reviewing, thus, how effectively we have followed each step of the presentation will contribute to further planning of even more effective methods. It is such thorough, overall planning which will lead to our improvement. Enthusiasm, attentiveness and fruitful learning are but a few of the fruits of such commitment.

Knowing our Children: A Top Priority

Our Christian learners are unique and individually created persons. Each is called to experience God now and forever more. Our task of helping this to happen is born out of our commitment to each, who is valued as precious, as singularly and totally loved by God. In the course of a lesson, the devoted catechist will, tactfully and gently, draw out of each learner the faith response which contributes to the budding relationship with God. Each will be led and challenged to one's maximum ability to respond in faith to what is being learned, to channel one's creativity in expressing what the heart has received.

Our children's educational and spiritual progress asks of us, for example, an appreciation of their need and hunger for sensory expression in the learning process. We will, then, meet them 'right where they are' in their need to concretize that which is abstract, and in their desire to make *real* that which the heart is gradually coming to know.

In understanding such needs, we will employ much color, various shapes, engaging rhythms, compelling symbols and all manner of visual, audio and other sensory resources to draw and hold youngsters' attention during their faith lessons. The learning environment will hold captivating sensory stimulation as, for example, we provide posters, large, bright banners, bulletin boards filled with interesting pictures, an inspiring prayer center, and numerous other attractive 'vehicles for the Truth to ride on.' Music tapes of children's liturgical songs become an integral part of learning, as do films, video tapes, excursions, large group celebrations and invited guests. All such sensory appeal will effectively contribute to the students' experiential process of receiving the truths of faith, and making them one's own. Many more examples of a stimulating environment and creative expressions of learning abound in the following chapters. What an exciting aspect of our own creativity toward the fostering and expressing of our children's growing faith!

So it is that the better we know our eager-believers, the more interesting and rewarding both teaching and learning become. How deeply we can enjoy the budding and growth of a child's faith! Together with their faith-centered home and family (a reality to which education ministries must continue to be dedicated) we work to reveal to them that, as seen in our actions and love, the living Lord is truly present in this day. Willing to be Christ's visual aid in their faith formation, we strive to represent His living reality in very ordinary ways. This tenderness finds us early-on, calling each by name, knowing something each is interested in (a sport, hobby, pet, etc.,) recognizing family members and having a cordial relationship with them. Our warm hand of friendship will be extended to each student, no matter how we feel about their attendance record or particular personality traits, should such seem unfavorable. All will be welcome both in our classroom, and in our heart. Our commitment to them will have us doing nothing less.

Our On-going Commitment to Catechetical Enrichment

The faith-full catechist will take advantage of opportunities offered on local and regional levels which, as we have said earlier, support our conviction that spiritual growth is essential to our ministry. From the small, more intimate staff meetings to area gatherings of catechists, we attend hoping, for example, to improve presentation skills, our understanding of children's faith development, and the application of constructive ideas which will support our catechetics. Whenever the proverbial "two or more" meet in His Name, there is a wealth of formation and information to be shared. Those with the treasure of many years of catechetical experience might seek out novices, offer their expertise and inspiration and, in turn, receive fresh enthusiasm from the encounter. We are life-givers, thereby one to the other, and to take part in enrichment is to keep alive our sense that ours is a shared ministry, deeply valued by others who are, likewise, called and committed.

Reading religious education periodicals and literature, using one's pastoral center's resource library, and dialoguing with leaders in the catechetical community all serve our needs for continual enrichment which nourishes our mind and heart and, ultimately, those of the children in our care.

Yes, commitment in a faith-full catechist costs. Commitment demands and expects time and energy from within us. Commitment anticipates that the catechist will, at times, respond farther, longer and fuller than might be requested in our basic job description. When such commitment to teach Christ is born in the heart, it feeds, supports and fertilizes and prepares for fruit much deep faith within us and within our children. In truth, we must be people with a "holy heartburn," as attested in Luke 24, a wonderful and productive state of health indeed!

COMPASSION

Together with the catechist's sense of conviction and commitment, a deep and abiding compassion must abound in our ministry to children. Compassion is another word for "true love" it is fuller and greater than even love to which we might give words. Compassion is heart-to-heart. In our serving, we are helping to bring a child's heart to the heart of God; we are seeing through his naturalness, her giftedness, his weaknesses, her 'childishness,' his sometimes naughtiness and uncooperativeness, her limitedness – in short, through all of their humanness to the child totally loved and redeemed by God and, thereby *worthy* of our true love, our compassion.

The faith-full catechist, with this initial mindset and heartset, will help to draw forth a child's faith more effectively because, responding to our compassion, one will

simply more readily believe that God's love is real and possible. Our compassion will have opened wider the child's faith-door. then, with ever more compassion, comes their challenge to own that faith and to live it.

In our compassion for children, our inter-relating will show concern for them as individuals. We will reach out with heart. We might offer one a shell for her collection, another encouraging words when attention is flagging. One's home situation might need our understanding, another's shyness might respond to our gentleness. Heart to heart, our caring reaches, touches and enkindles what longs to come to life in them. Thus, compassion "walks with another on the road" and, delightfully discovers that "it is the Lord" all the while.

At times compassion will ask of us a thoroughgoing adjustment to the child with life's special difficulties and challenges. Be it the wheel-chair bound, the attention-deficient, the learning impaired, or another special-needs youngster, they come before us with the same open-hearted expectation and potential for empowerment as their fellows. Compassion finds us responding in sensitive and practical ways which allow faith to flourish steadily in such individual situations.

With compassionate love, which makes us aware of children's needs, our lessons will hold, as we have emphasized, necessary sensory involvement, tactile experiences and creative expression correspondent to their learning level. Is, then, teaching compassionately truly catechizing? Overwhelmingly, "Yes!" for meeting children thus is truly loving them unconditionally, and with the very love of Christ pervading our teaching. Through such cooperation with the Holy Spirit, we can be confident that, as children use their natural gifts for learning, their efforts will surely be rewarded. With our compassion on their behalf they truly will be.

CONVERSION

Perhaps the most challenging hallmark of the faith-full catechist is the fourth "C" of Conversion. Here, we will unfold conversion as a much wider concept than a one-time, radical change of heart in a religious experience. Conversion, in its deeper sense, involves our on-going, reshaping, often reconstructing, of our whole person in the process of conforming more surely to the personality of Christ Our Lord. Conversion in this context will, essentially, occur continually throughout all of our lifetime. We can rightly consider ourselves, then, as constantly being reborn, being transformed, as repeatedly undergoing a kind of inner metamorphosis. Indeed, of all the "good news," perhaps this is the best news!

Blessed with the gift of faith, we are called not only to know God, but, more deeply, to know that God knows us. There is, in this divinely initiated relationship, no limit to the potentiality of our conversion! However, being earth-bound, limited, and quite imperfect, we are all too often confronted with our own unchangingness. The journey home seems incessantly marked with potholes of our selfishness, and the side-roads of indifference to progress and inner growth. Yet, the Spirit of God within us persists. Each day is new, with invitation to go forward, to advance strong and purposeful in virtue, simply believing in the One who lovingly awakens us to the possibilities of true growth.

Perhaps at times, 'full sanctity,' even as an ideal, sometimes seems neigh impossible or even improbable for us. In all honesty we may be very comfortable on the spiritual level of the present time. No need for worry, here, if this is our lot, for the Lord surely delights in letting us discover the truth in ourselves, and in helping us to wrestle with and to overcome the many barriers in our path of conversion. His 'work' in us is always life-generating. All that is needed for the flow of His power to begin at every turn is our mustard seed of faith. What a hope we can take comfort in along the journey!

Yet, as the Letter of James would tell us (James 2:14,) faith must be accompanied by action. Our whole person must express our belief. Action lived out of one's willingness – yes, eagerness – must mark His disciples. by feeding the hungry, comforting the sorrowing, befriending the lonely, by praying for the living and the dead, counseling the doubtful – all the *doing* of what are familiarly known as the Corporal and Spiritual Works of Mercy – we are lifting those words off the page and imprinting them on the palms of our hands. We are letting them spring from the depth of ourselves. Here is where authentic, genuine faith comes alive! Every gesture of love in our everyday walk can be a living word! These "works," and every other verb in the gospels, call the faith-full catechist to be a person who hears Christ's two most compelling words: "Come" and "Go." They fit together, are connected, are one call. Therefore, our action/answers need to come from deep within the pocket of our integrity not from merely the head, nor only from one's heart, but from the very soul of our central being. And isn't the price of such response nothing less than one's whole self? Therefore, in arising from our very depth, our merciful works will be ever as genuine and sincere as was Christ's own. It is from this depth within us that He can lead the way for our conversion.

"Listen to Nature"

The unlimited treasures in Nature – those wonderfully available gifts and ordinary encounters around us in every season – can aid our understanding of a spiritual concept such as conversion. These free gifts are ready to help if we could be open to their messages. For example, we might sit reflectively before a simple bowl of water, or observe it flowing into the open hands. Here the gift reminds us of how water continually converts our food, our health and the very environment in which we live. Our meditation can easily flow into an awareness of Baptism and its gift of potential for conversions being symbolically 'poured' upon us.

Contemplating a handful of seed, or actually planting them, can wrap us in thought about their conversion, their dying and coming into new life, indeed life on a more glorious level in the process. Herein, we can be led to recognize and rejoice in our own times of exchanging Self for the new empowerment in loving generously and freely. The lowly seed's message is the invitation to conversion, to become the promised "more" hidden in the "letting go," when we, too, would heed the call of the Gardener.

Another visual aid filled with imagery possibilities is the unlighted/lighted candle. Behold the conversion when its self-giving, *which alone draws out its inner beauty,* becomes the powerful conversion image. How easily we are led to "see" in the burning candle the process of our own transformation in Christ when we, willingly ignited by the Spirit, burn with love in our whole being.

These, and other simple images in Nature, can bring us close to the spiritual realities deep within for which we intuitively hunger to understand, such as birth, life, becoming, growth, enlightenment, death and resurrection. Seek out and enjoy Nature's images. Our faith-fullness as a catechist can depend in a large measure upon our willingness to be touched by their conversion messages.

THE BLESSINGS IN INCOMPLETENESS

Walking with children on their faith journey, companioning them as a faith-full catechist, will always ask superlatives of us: intense conviction, unflagging commitment, profound compassion, and continual conversion. Indeed these signs of life mark us as responding wholeheartedly to Our Lord's call to "bring the little ones unto me." So, called, sent forth and sustained in His power, we can confidently expect our efforts on their behalf to lead them safely on their path to full life in Him. Together we can rejoice in His abundant grace toward this purpose.

However, despite our genuine experience of faith, and sincere efforts at completion in our reationship with Christ, we realitically conclude that, alas, we are not yet wholly faith-full. And not yet wholly holy! There is always the more in the invitation. More of our hearing the call, more of our responsive discipleship, more of our dedication to Him as a children's catechist.

This reality, though, needs but to encourage us to continually reach for the ever higher ground of our personal faith-fullness. For at each turn on the path at every increasing grade of terrain, Christ Himself meets us, offering His "more," so that we can embrace our own "being more." What a glorious plan is our unfinishedness! What joy, then, is in our quest as a children's catechist, for ever more faith-fullness!

Faith begins
not in the word
and the concept
but in the image
and the symbol.
Before faith is credible to reason
it must be credible
to the imagination.

John Henry Cardinal Newman

CHAPTER 3

SETTING THE SCENE: YOUR GATHERING SPACE

Two weeks before the third graders were scheduled to begin meeting regularly for their religious education classes, each of them received from their catechist a letter and one piece of a Bible story puzzle. The letter, which enthusiastically welcomed each child and previewed some of their learning activities for the coming year, invited each one to bring in the enclosed puzzle piece to the first class. There, the letter explained, each person would add their important help in making the puzzle picture complete. The catechist, aware that the mailing would spark the children's interest and curiosity was also sending them an unspoken message about the 'climate' which they could anticipate in their classroom, in their 'space.' Such personal reaching out to students could project only a positive learning atmosphere, one conducive to the building up of both the child's mind and spirit.

And on their first day of class the children's enthusiasm was amply rewarded, with the room's hospitality and arrangements exceeding their expectations. On the door a *"Welcome"* sign was decorated with bright paper balloons bearing their names. Bulletin boards were filled with large pictures of Jesus and his apostles. A "wonder" table held dozens of scavenged Nature treasures, inviting their interest and their touch. Several eight-inch wide paper streamers which were hung both horizontally and vertically, compelled attention with their brightly-lettered, memory-jogging questions. In an open area of the room, a circle of chairs waited for the young occupants. Large tables were 'set' for a hands-on activity which would climax the lesson. The catechist's gentle yet firm voice greeted the children, and directed them to the table where the picture puzzle frame awaited their vital piece. Hospitality? Order? A sense of purpose? Surely, these qualities, and more, are evident when the gathering space is ready for learning and spiritual discovery.

Your gathering space – that particular place where you and your students meet to learn, to pray, to believe, to create and to encounter God – is your Mt. Horeb; indeed, your holy ground, for there God will be sought, revealed, listened to and more fully known. Let us look upon this as the truly sacred place it is. This being so, your space will be for the children a home away from home, a place where they can be as they are before God: open-hearted, free, curious, eager, receptive. Let their gathering space, therefore, be a place of light and comfort and, above all, life!

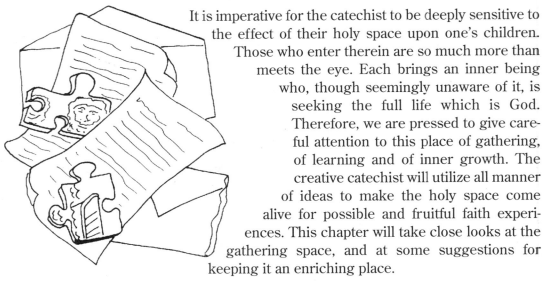

A student's invitation includes a puzzle piece to bring in for completing the waiting puzzle in the classroom.

It is imperative for the catechist to be deeply sensitive to the effect of their holy space upon one's children. Those who enter therein are so much more than meets the eye. Each brings an inner being who, though seemingly unaware of it, is seeking the full life which is God. Therefore, we are pressed to give careful attention to this place of gathering, of learning and of inner growth. The creative catechist will utilize all manner of ideas to make the holy space come alive for possible and fruitful faith experiences. This chapter will take close looks at the gathering space, and at some suggestions for keeping it an enriching place.

"GETTING TO KNOW YOU; GETTING TO KNOW ALL ABOUT YOU"

Gathering spaces are likely as varied in shape and size and character as the parish situations in which they are found. One's area might be a shared classroom, a place for full-time education as well as for religious education classes held during other hours. Another space might be a multi-purpose room, where a number of groups share its accommodations. Yet another might be located in a home, such as part of one's basement area. Still another space might be the answer to every catechist's prayer: a large, well-lighted room all your own! With walls of bulletin boards and inviting blackboards. And with some carpeting, childsized chairs, activity tables and a sink (while we're making our wish list!). However, the essential matter about your space isn't its perfection. What is critical in the name of religious education and children's faith development is *what you make of the given space,* how you use it, fill it, maximize its potential. Every space can become stimulating and life-giving. Every space invites our creativity and sensitivity.

Really get to 'know' your space. Imagine what you could bring to it to make it an atmosphere in which shapes, colors, movement and dimensions are utilized to express their messages. What will you hang up, post, suspend or display to capture and hold attention? How will your space invite, welcome and compel children to want to return to it? Let your ingenuity come into full play, using your understanding about a viable learning environment which children need for faith learning to blossom. Our excitement can be as that of a competent interior decorator: we should take what we have, capitalize on its virtues and proceed to create its possibilities.

WHAT HELPS TO SAY "C'MON IN!"

Preparing our space calls for awareness of certain 'messages' given in it, such as those with the use of bright colors, particular styles of lettering and the placement of centers for times of listening, creating and praying. Above all, this "setting the scene" asks our deep compassion our "feeling with" for the children's needs educationally, physically and spiritually. Compassion asks us to wonder what it feels like to be in our space, to see it through the eyes of our children. The more informed and aware the catechist is about the needs pertaining to one's particular age group, the more appealing and effective one will make their gathering space. So, be ready to do whatever it will take to bring life and character into their sacred space.

How, then, do children relate to their gathering place. . .how do they feel about, and respond to, the given area? Our insights here are critical to creating a place which will be perceived in a most positive light. Perhaps their initial moments in it will set the tone for attentiveness and participation. Let's consider some necessities for helping this to happen.

Children of all ages thrive in an atmosphere of recognition and acceptance, where they feel valued and considered. There is "something about the place" into which a child is willing to go and to learn. In such a space, the catechist greets each by name and/or a pleasant, positive comment. What wonders a kindly compliment, some personal praise and a caring comment can accomplish in the child! Early arrivers are made to feel needed and valued by being asked to do a helpful task before the others join them. Watch children become more eager to participate when they have received your warm hospitality. Notice their readiness to cooperate once their presence has been acknowledged. It's true, too, that the first several moments of our hospitality give nonverbal clear 'vibes' about our sensitivity toward them. These "greeting moments" clearly help children to sense the room's positive emotional climate, a 'weather forecast' essential to their growth. (During these moments, we are simply living out the Golden Rule for we, as adults, enjoy and appreciate personal recognition in a group situation, also. Let our sensitivity be passed on.)

Whenever their catechist is present to them in a warm, receptive manner, children gain a strong feeling of emotional stability. "Someone really cares. I'm being paid attention." What child is not the more inspired for having been made to feel special in some way?

Our very body language often telegraphs to them, too. Facial expressions, tones of voice, stance – all can positively magnify children into attentiveness, learning and further participation as the lesson progresses. It is when they do have this "good feeling about the place," as well as about their catechist, that students can feel connected to the learning and to its purpose for them.

TAPPING INTO THE POWER OF HEALTHY ORDERLINESS

Another first impression which children intuit is a space's orderliness or its lack thereof. Order in a room is not necessarily sterile perfection where one moves or speaks only on cue. We strive for a healthy sense of order, which should be reflected naturally in our person and our space; one which children surely will both see and intuit. Peace and harmony are the companions of a room's sensible visual order, as seen in a systematic seating arrangement, prepared learning materials and ready visual aids which are consistent with the 'flow' of the lesson. Children sense healthy structure in tangible signs of some continuity between several consecutive lessons, also. Such evidence might be made clear, for example, to First Communion students as they see the parts of the Mass entitled on large, poster-paper "chunks of bread," the culmination of which become an entire "loaf," readily understandable as each of the pieces is mounted (lesson-by-lesson) on a long sheet of brighly-colored butcher paper, and the whole "loaf" is, then, posted in a prominent place to enjoy. Herein, the pieces, or steps, create a sensible "whole." Continuity proceeds to a logical conclusion, minus unhealthy confusion.

Stepping into a room which evinces harmony, constancy and healthy order, youngsters can allow themselves to relax, and to trust, and to be necessarily receptive. Much thoughtfulness, indeed, needs to be given in the catechist creating the influential orderliness of their effective gathering space.

CLARIFYING WITH THE "BIG PICTURE"

Young students 'connect' more easily with what is being presented when they can comprehend the overall purpose of the given learning time. Therefore, part of their initial orientation ought to be some helpful awareness in visual or auditory form of the lesson's subject matter. This sense of awareness, too, is part of the order which is essential for learning, and which should be offered to them. One tactic which will quickly capture attention and set the lesson's purpose in mind is that of printing the lesson's title on a colorfully-lettered, butcher-paper 'banner,' or simply on a blackboard, using rainbow lines of colored chalk. Another arresting way to announce the theme is to allow a fairly large stuffed animal to hold a sign which tells all about it. Attention holding? Remember, as a creative catechist, you will extend your effort and resources into every available direction, so that your holy space really does become a place of interest and life for young learners. In this important process of setting the scene, we might well ask ourselves a few self-revealing questions regarding the atmosphere and impression of our particular learning place.

Do I enjoy coming into our gathering space? (If not, why not?)
How will I look, sound and act really receptive to each child?
How will I greet them as they arrive? Have I learned their names?
What specific expectations await them once they have entered?
What first impressions will the children, and parents, receive?
What will greet their senses when they arrive and are oriented?
What evidences of their learning, discussions, activities are clearly apparent
    as helps to memory and review?
Where will they go in the changing movements during the lesson?

LETTING 'SIGNS' IN YOUR SPACE TELL THEIR MESSAGES

It might well be repeated that our gathering space for religious education is a holy place, and it will be all the more so if we bring into it certain 'signs' which will tell them this is so. A crucifix hung at eye level, perhaps surrounded with appropriate seasonal decorations of autumn wheat, evergreen branches or spring (silk) flowers will give this primary symbol life-giving significance. Many tasteful pictures of the Lord and familiar gospel scenes can be encountered easily when grouped on a bulletin board or at any available eye level place. Pictures 'speak' messages often stronger and more impressive than words do. Keep interest high by changing them occasionally, entitling scripturally, and mounting them on bright colors of art paper.

ESSENTIAL FOR BUILDING FAITH: THE PRAYER PLACE

The learning space is most complete when the 'sign' of an attractive prayer place is included in it. Will yours be a special table? A designated corner? A large portable, covered box? Let your prayer place, however adaptable, be reflective of the current liturgical season, its contents as simple or as dramatic as the mood of the period might dictate.

Begin with a low table. Invite the youngsters to decorate a pretty prayer cloth, to add a broad ribbon reflecting the liturgical season, and to bring in fresh flowers, greens or a plant. Add a statue or picture of the Risen Lord, a bowl of fresh water, an open Bible and a simple candle. Especially during October (the month of the Holy Rosary) and May (the month of Mary,) add several rosaries to the table. Such a significant setting can also offer children contact with traditional Christian symbols, which might be carved into the candle, or drawn onto the prayer cloth in lovely colors. Children will be naturally attracted to such an area in your holy space for moments of quiet reflection and interior harmony. Such an atmosphere for group prayer will more easily draw in and hold their attentiveness.

"SPACE SWEET SPACE"

A colorful fabric banner invites children's delight, a they "see as person rejoicing" by peering at it with eyes slightly closed

One particular guideline which will be valued in providing for children's faith learning place is: *let the space truly reflect the children in it.* Let it show their interests, their level of development, and, above all, *their* contributions to its 'look.' What enormous pleasure and educational value children gain when they are surrounded with what they have created or have arranged! How they delight in seeing their own artwork displayed, their pictures tacked on bulletin boards. What fun to see their own Bible stories dangling from a clothesline. Such space becomes, rightly, *theirs!* It feeds their interest and inspiration when children set out their clay baskets of 'bread and fish,' their journals, scrapbooks or hand puppets of gospel characters on a table ready for appreciation and sharing. It invites healthy pride in one's unique addition to a "Creation Story" mural in process. And, most importantly, such a space promotes necessary ownership, where a sense of responsibility is fostered and allowed to thrive. Let's anticipate manifold rewards from our efforts to provide as dynamic a faith-space as possible.

Because most children have a natural urge to compete, it is wise to avoid displaying choice items only, thus singling out 'good' from 'otherwise' from student's creations. When they do see everyone's activities displayed, they catch the specialness of each, in a growing spirit of mutual charity. Love competeth not . . .

THE FRUIT IN MUTUALLY SHARED SPACE

Whatever might be your space situation, it asks for creative harmony with other fellow space-sharers. If you share in classroom space with another group, work out a compatible system of utilizing surfaces and floor areas. Decide mutually on an arrangement for storage, displays, common properties and prep times. Sharing one's space asks, too, a show of forgiveness after infractions occur, and a building up of renewed trust in one another. Thus do we witness to our students a genuine graciousness being lived within the Body of Christ. Surely, too, new life and deeper faith often grow out of the seeds of such practicality.

"THE PAUSE THAT REFRESHES"

At times when children enter their learning space following a play period, or an otherwise stimulating activity, they will need a few moments to quiet down, to detach from their former animation. The gathering place can help them 'switch gears' physically and mentally when some peaceful instrumental music greets them as they arrive and begin to reorient themselves. When soft lights and mellow sounds draw them in, children simply, can more easily focus on our presentation. The creative catechist will build up a small collection of appealing audio tapes from which to draw on days when everyone needs to first absorb the peace and harmony of a soothing atmosphere. Such a time of quieting one's thought and "getting my whole self ready to learn" will benefit everyone present.

"WHERE MIGHT WE GO FROM HERE?"

It is characteristic of young children – and often of those in the middle grades – to want a change of scenery, and to need some physical movement within the classroom within an extended period of time. Monotony and boredom will have no invitations into their space when we occasionally provide for a change of location and some purposeful movement. For example, having sat attentively for fifteen or twenty minutes, the youngsters are given a (creative?) stretch break. Their thoughts will more easily stay on task if, as they stretch limbs they are invited to "think thank-thoughts" for their senses. During another flexing time, they might "become trees blowing in the strong wind, or hungry lions prowling and stomping around the jungle." Encourage imagination, too, when it flavors their indoors-time in inclement weather. And doesn't the moment taken invigorate their catechist, too?

Further, changing 'stations' within the room can given everyone a sense of freshness. For instance, after a group has been sitting for the first part of the lesson, they will enjoy standing at a table for a creative activity and later, sitting cross-legged on the floor for their prayer time. Change is a healthy ingredient in a teaching plan, one to which confident students quite readily respond. The space-conscious catechist will adapt the area to the young children's need for such motion and change of location when it is beneficial.

BRINGING SPACE TO LIFE, AND LIFE TO SPACE

Being quite well oriented to the space, and having a sense of its importance in the scheme of faith formation, walk now, if you will, into your space once again. Play with some of these ideas, in your mind's eye. Consider some of these ideas for enlivening it. Imagine some of your own and "see" them as lively possibilities

Print faith concepts and related Scripture verses on long strips of computer roll ends. Use clear, large and bright lettering for unmistakable visibility. Tape or tack them up in the form of a border around the learning area or circle the room for impact. Display them for reading diagonally, too. Great for any learning atmosphere, and for a handy review reference.

Let the eye play with three-dimensional visual aids, such as those suspended from strung wire or perhaps from light fixtures. For example, three large, white poster board discs attached vertically with colorful yarn ties were hung in a First Communion classroom. On both sides of the top disk was lettered EUCHARIST. Likewise, on the center disk was MEANS. And on the bottom disk was THANK YOU GOD. Each was printed in large eye catching fluorescent colors. As the slightest breeze caught the large, communion-shaped disks, they moved freely, twirling each under the one above it, and inviting readers to 'play the message' in multi-colored splendor. Such suspended truths are sure to 'stick' well in young minds. Others, such as colored hearts bearing bright lettering of HOLINESS IS WHOLENESS, or HOLINESS IS A BEATITUDE ATTITUDE compellingly prompt middlegraders' thoughts. As with other teaching aids, clarity and simplicity are our guides in these creations.

Suspend a lovely, "teaching" waterfall for Baptism lessons. On a long length of blue butcher paper to be hung vertically, entitle the fall GOD GIVES US WATER. Beneath this add colorful pictures of people enjoying water. Print under these: TO ENJOY. Continue down the fall with pictures of people using water (for washing, bathing, etc.) under which is printed TO USE. Next add pictures of people eating, of foods from a garden, a tea bag, a real package of fruit drink mix and any other items or illustrations of life-giving uses of water. Under them print: AND TO BRING LIFE. Plan for enough length of waterfall to now extend over a card table beneath it, with THANK YOU, GOD, FOR WATER lettered at the very bottom of it. To emphasize the spiritual connotation of water to Baptism, set a bowl of water, a pitcher, a candle, a white 'robe,' some oil in a small dish and a true-to-life Baptismal certificate or two on the card-table. When such a visual display is hung high in the room, with the table receiving its allowance, such a message will be repeatedly encountered again and again.

Blow up a bevy of balloons and tape them up around the room. Their instant color and captivating form suggests festivity, and will quickly lift young spirits when a 'delight break' is in order. Write attention-getting statements on them with felt markers: learnings for review, probing questions or new vocab being built. One favorite with primary children is a huge, red, heart-shaped balloon bobbing in the center of their prayerplace quite instinctively they "name" it GOD, and enjoy the tangible inference of the symbol in their midst.

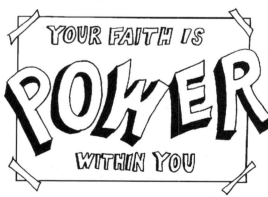

Extended lettering offers more visual impact

Draw messages from healthy plants in your 'space.' Arrange several plants in places near the children's activity area and prayer place for their strong visual witness of God's work upon seed, of the blessing which water is to plants, and of the beauty which plants provide for us. Have a planting party for your 'space' when a variety of seeds (brought in by the children) are lovingly buried, and whose new life is later celebrated. Enjoy bulbs, corms and shoots, too.

Hang large, brightly-lettered butcher paper banners around the room announcing a piece of "Good News" from the Scriptures or a Truth being learned. Let these remind, prompt and challenge learners. Use the eye-catching fluorescent colors in key words of the messages. (For example: the words YOUR FAITH IS and POWER WITHIN YOU!) Enlarge certain words and play with their spacing. Try out various styles of lettering for their graphic impact. Rejoice in the lasting impressions these visuals make!

The creative catechist will 'know' the gathering space intimately. You will know its areas which wait to be filled with large, colorful Christian graphics and suspended messages, where sturdy wire or string can be attached for the hanging of children's (or your own!) creativity. You will know the possibilities for mobility within the given space and classtime.

Knowing one's space well, and being willing to creatively construct an atmosphere foster faith and be interesting is, indeed, a primary challenge within our call. And what marvelously stimulating rewards are in store when we meet our space's challenge, for in the 'knowing' of our space lies the power for its effectiveness.

IN THE SPACE FOR CHILDREN'S LITURGY OF THE WORD

When children are invited to celebrate Liturgy of the Word on their level of understanding during Mass, their gathering place ought to be one where creative worship is possible. Here they will listen to and implant the Word of God in their hearts. In this place they are drawn to celebrate, and to bring to life, what God is saying to them today. It is to this purpose that their gathering space be sensitively created. Whether it be an entire room, or but a corner in a larger space, the area needs to help children carry out their 'work' of listening peacefully and quietly. To the greatest possible extent, everything about their worship place should reflect the very purpose of their gathering: celebrating the Word of God. What, then, might such a space look like, and 'feel' like?

A seating arrangement of benches or chairs set around a small table will offer them necessary closeness to the table of the Word. This nearness will suggest the affinity and community which God desires His people to know while He speaks to them. It also simply helps children to focus more closely on the objects of their worship, thus attracting and holding their attention more certainly.

The prayer table is covered with a white cloth, preferably one which reaches to the floor. A broad ribbon reflecting the current liturgical season's color is laid over the cloth. A large, stout candle on the table helps to make the strong statement that Jesus, who speaks, is the Light of the World, and it is He in our midst. An open Bible, or the very Children's Lectionary behind which they processed into the space, is placed in the center of the table in an upright position. Thus, visually, the 'table is set' for the nourishing which will be offered to the young hearers of the Word.

Bright and beautiful support materials ought to be clearly visible to all, mounted near, and preferably surrounding, the children. A large wheel of the Church's seasons in the liturgical year can be posted and referred to from time to time. Large, colorful banners might be hung, bearing such proclamations as HAPPY

ARE WE WHO HEAR, THE WORD OF GOD AND KEEP IT IN OUR HEART, or PRAISE TO YOU, LORD JESUS CHRIST, or perhaps, simply, ALLELUIA! Children intuit the value in seeing and reading such expressions, which add to their purpose in gathering. Variety and changes in such visual environment will help to sustain participation and interest for young hearts, too.

A nearby black (or white) board, or a large pad of newsprint set on an easel, is convenient for imprinting the day's Responsorial Psalm. Space here, too, can be made for the children's Prayers of the Faithful at their time of sharing intentions and joining in their response.

This space further aids children during their worship of the Word of God when it includes certain visual aids which are carried over from past celebrations. Banners or posters proclaiming former hearings which remain in the room for a few weeks help them recall what they have heard. These can prompt some sharing of how the Word has been lived out in their lives. Such refreshing of their memories also gives a sense of continuity to the regular gathering and its purpose.

Special celebrations of the Word will take on fuller meaning when the worship space allows for time of, for example, processions, the crowning of Mary, or the building up of an Advent-to-Epiphany manger scene. The creative catechist will be sensitive to the enriching possibilities which can be opened up in the sacred space for Children's Liturgy of the Word.

When components such as these are made sensitively part of their celebration, children feel assisted in opening up to their faith. It is out of such a supported framework that a deep level of worship and participation can be enjoyed. In such a setting, children come to anticipate and appropriate the Word of God, since it has been made meaningful to them.

"HIDDEN MESSAGES" IN ANY CHILDREN'S LEARNING

As it has been said, any space where children's faith is being nurtured is sacred space. This actuality should call forth all the sensitivity and creativity the catechist can summon. Understanding that children need their gathering space to be one where they can intuit Spirit-life, and where they can feel 'at home,' one will go to great creative lengths to meet those needs. In love and compassion for the learners, one will feed and nurture them as the developing people of God which they are. One's students will be known as well as possible, respected in their growth (or lack thereof) and encouraged in faith-steps through and in an atmosphere most conducive for them to advance.

Children instinctively hunger for such compassion from adults. They come to us expecting to be included, desiring to be involved, hoping to be filled and generally willing for some learning to happen. It is a truly awesome responsibility for us to make their learning space an inviting, hospitable, encouraging and enlivening place. Yet, what other kind would we choose for them?

Yes, even the building entrance into their space should draw children in. What, we might well ask, is there to welcome them? (Or will they see but the EXIT sign?) As they enter, will they encounter interesting pictures, posters or even photographs of themselves as the special people they are? Might they pause around a "Birthday people" bulletin board, or one of "News About Families?" Will they find their names on an "Attendance Recognition!" notice? What will remind everyone to celebrate certain religious holidays or Saints' feast days? These first impressions can and do set a definitive tone to their place of learning. Such signs of *life* warmly draw children into their learning atmosphere. Such symbols of our caring and ministering will surely compel children to enter into their sacred space, and help them to feel a part of what is happening there.

When we enter
into the world
of a child
we need not think
we are "lowering ourselves."
Instead, and indeed,
it asks a raising up
within ourselves
of a childlike heart
that we may meet on the ground of
pure faith and dance to the music
of its possibilities.

Ruth Ann Rost

CALLING FORTH FAITH BY WAY OF THE SENSES

A group of ten- and eleven-year-old children are celebrating the Sacrament of Reconciliation. They have gathered with their parents for prayer, for private confession and for a meaningful experience of God's forgiveness in a personal, relevant way. They have each held a small stone, and, during the consideration of it as a symbol of how our 'heart' can become 'hard and cold and concealing of its beauty,' each prayerfully recognized and renounced the selfishness and sin which had closed their heart to God's loving plan for them. Following their private time with the priest, each then dropped his/her stone into a bright red, heart-shaped bucket (seen as a fitting symbol of God) and accepted immediately, from a colorfully decorated potted white branch in front of the parish Paschal candle, a brightly colored, soft, felt, heart ornament – a fitting symbol of the new heart now within them. This simple keepsake speaks to the interior child of love, forgiveness, conversion and a new beginning in the Lord.

Several grade-school age boys and girls have completed their preparation for initiation into the Church. They are happily creating a banner which they will hang for the celebration. On it are cutout letters forming the compelling message: *I have called you by name, you are mine* Isaiah 43:1.

Surrounding the Scripture are the children's large, handprinted names, each artistically rendered to show the child's name "spoken as lovingly as God's voice heard by the child." The children will rejoice in the sight of their banner, realizing that God has, indeed, called them as individually as they have depicted the sound of their own name within their heart.

A group of third-graders had been discussing the parable of the Good Samaritan. They had pondered its meanings, and probed for reasons why Jesus had told such a story. Now, deeply impressed with its message, they were compiling the parable's incidences and sequence by making a horizontal strip of the story, each student drawing a portion of the event. They eagerly planned to tape

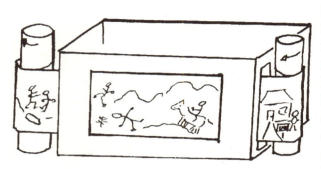

A sturdy cardboard box becomes a viewing screen for unrolling a story created by young interpreturs.

their 'pieces' of the parable together and roll the long strip through a cut-out screen on their 'homemade video box.' Each felt the importance of his/her contribution to the arresting project. Thus do the senses lead the child's faith, and help to welcome the Truth into their heart.

APPRECIATING THE HALLMARKS OF CHILDHOOD

Someone has humorously quipped that young children operate on two basic principles:

(1) *Never spill on a dirty floor* and
(2) *More is never enough*

Anyone who has watched the pouring of fruit juice at the open refrigerator door, or the applying of glue in the creating of an art project, will verify these words. They do belie a free-spiritedness which we all at one time held so dear in the Land of Childhood.

Although, as adults, we have gradually grown from a life of dependency and have, with sustained effort, loosened the protective shell of "me," we can, however, reflect upon our own somewhat laborious journey through the tenuous terrain as a time when "it took a lot of slow to grow." This insight gives us, as a creative catechist, much reason for learning all we can about this wonderful and mysterious time. Our children are in its embrace. Our appreciation of their characteristics during these years will guide our effectiveness in drawing forth and building up their faith. The more we know children as the processors of life's experiences which they are, the better we can interrelate and enjoy them – and the more completely can we call forth their growth in faith.

Do we not marvel at the most obvious characteristic of children: their playfulness? We say that it "comes naturally" for them, and we are in awe at their abandon to its power! By the age of six, a child is an uninhibited expert at playing. Their powers of imitating, imagining and creating help them to express and celebrate who they are! Indeed, they often reveal a freedom and spontaneity which we might well envy! Play opens up to children the wonders and powers of their very self-ness, of their existence. Their natural tendency to dramatize, characterize and personalize action helps children to identify with their world. We look for and rejoice in their playfulness and well might we, their catechist, learn (re-learn?) their secrets for freeing up our own natural creativity, the better to help our children develop the whole person, the cognitive and the creative.

So keenly does the primary child respond to what is happening around one that all of life seems a cause for celebration. With verbalizing and reacting physically the child is compelled to make a contribution to the "action." While we do take joy in this enthusiasm for living, it is with great sensitivity and care, however, that we need to provide guidelines and direction which will promote their healthy learning and development. Simply, their creative energy needs to be channeled toward wholesome endeavors.

Throughout primary childhood, it is the five senses which serve as one's chief learning avenues. These powerful 'tools' help to compile information, satisfy curiosity and experience ever deeper levels of learning. Already in love with life, children touch, taste, see, hear and smell all of its available components, continually adding data to their store of awareness, wonder and amazement. A given day seems all too brief when so much life awaits to be 'sensed,' when the world so tantalizingly invites one's handling, listening, eating, aroma-checking and watching! We appreciate this truth, as with sincere devotion we plan for and present the realm of the spirit unto them. It is in this light of the role that the child's senses play in learning that we, as creative catechists, welcome their exuberance and help them awaken to a rich, full life of faith.

It is nothing less than delightful to watch high-spirited youngsters come into their classroom. They seem to use their whole body, every wiggly limb, to express thought and feelings sometimes falling into a seat, rolling and stretching on a carpet, pumping the raised hand vigorously to answer a question. Their joy in movement "shows and tells" their joy for life! Let us capitalize on this natural receptivity and energy which children bring to their learning time. (See the preceding chapter for ideas on helping their environment 'come alive' for active learners.)

THE COMFORT OF THE PRESENT TENSE

Young children characteristically seem compelled to live in the now. What is immediate receives their energy and attention. What is happening currently arrests interest. In their limitedness, they engage totally in the present moment, for consequence and results often have not yet taken firm stands in their value system. "Now" is safe. "Now" is reliable, acceptable, in itself demanding what can be given by the child. We goal-oriented adults might feel disconcerted with such compulsion, yet with compassion we allow for the process of learning to happen, lest by imposing our haste we would ultimately shatter that spontaneity so vital in the process. As children develop learning skills, it is more feasible (they will discover) to see with a longer range of vision the particular outcome of an activity. Children in middle-childhood (ages 9 to 12) typically comprehend more wholeness in a task, and see the process as valuable in itself, and contributing to the overall aim. What is of importance to us here is our need for sensitivity to young children's natural impulses and developmental changes in regard to creative expression.

CREATIVITY SATISFIES CHILDREN

"Let's make something!" What, we might wonder, is the inherent value of any creative activity to the learning child? How do their sensory, tactile, creative expressions contribute to their learning and necessary development? Moreover, and critical to the creative catechist, how might we incorporate this contribution into the child's experiences of faith learning?

Children are innately creative. They make something for the sheer joy of it. Their creativity grows with every stage of discovery and curiosity. Feeling, seeing, hearing, smelling and tasting, as we have seen, is part of healthy development, for sensing satisfies the urge to know the world around them, consequently to discover it more intimately, to 'own' it. The five senses become doors to this discovery. As they are opened, the child sees how one can understand and partake in their world. Such important insights impel them to express unique ideas about what is sensed. Therein, the child opens up to one's God-given gift of creativity!

Some children create to communicate deep feelings, to relive vivid experiences or to simply record an impression. Often the literary and graphic arts serve as the typical creative outlets for expressing such feelings so essential to their emotional health. Too, many children find intense satisfaction in the dramatic arts, 'playing' particular roles to identify with. Creative activities allow children to "find their place," to identify themselves and sometimes to try to solve difficult situations. Making something builds up self-confidence and gives one the feeling of being successful at a task, as well as encourages further attempts to achieve, all valid reasons for giving children much opportunity and leeway for the natural, creative self-expression needed for growth.

Contributing in added ways to healthy emotional development, a child's creativity can help 'let off steam' and overcome frustration. Dramatic play, for example, is a wholesome avenue for communicating feelings and restoring self-respect in a hurt child. Creativity can be just the right medicine for a child's ill ego.

Through a painting, an original story, or a child-crafted dramatic play, a child can express precious dreams, wishes and hopes. For a brief time he can live in the world of the imagination and fantasy, experiencing healthful escapes into his own interior terrain.

It is no small deed to encourage children to discover and enjoy their natural creativity. Self-confidence, inner strength and courage are but a few of the desirable qualities we can help children to build through creative accomplishments. Sadly, where creativity has been discouraged or neglected, this important part of one's wholeness seldom will be made up after childhood. As stake in our response to children's needs for creative expression and sensory involvement is their very dignity as fully integrated people who uninhibitedly communicate their own unique relationship to the world. In this, we bring them to some truth about themselves. Creative expression helps them reveal and highly value that which is within them. We help children to know how good it is to do something for the love of it, and to own the conviction that the doing is indeed good.

CHILDLIKE QUALITIES: JOY

Really, is it any wonder that Jesus so loved the children whom He befriended? What was it He saw in them to endear them so? Perhaps a look with our sensitive eyes will reveal those characteristics. In addition to their passion for play and compulsion for creativity, young children are for the most part, guileless, frank and honest. We witness, too, their inclination to be literal in interpreting situations. In a word, we might call them very *real* people. These awesome qualities delight us! And they can truly inspire us. Perhaps in these is their blessing to us as I have perceived in many situations over my catechist years.

Within a lesson about the Eucharist, a group of second-graders was invited to tell why we come to church to receive Jesus on Sunday. One confident young student suggested, "Because by Saturday we kind of run out of Jesus." And to my profound delight, he immediately added, ". . . but, no matter how much Jesus we take, He *never* runs out!" I simply thought ". . . of such is the Kingdom." Literal? "Real"?

When their pastor dropped in to visit, he invited the children to "ask me whatever is on your mind." Hands flew! This catechist thought that surely this would provide some in depth understanding about, say, Jesus' presence in Communion or, perhaps, our important role in the Church. After all, here was Father C. who would helpfully explain such important matters with the children. More hands. Could there be that many questions? Then the pastor, with exceeding gentleness, fielded such *important* questions as:

1. Father, why do you wear black?
2. Father, are you nervous before Mass?
3. Father, what do you do on your day off?

Then there was the six-year-old boy who had just returned to the pew after accompanying his mother to Communion. He observed her with her head bowed, quietly giving thanks. Then, brimming with curiosity, he leaned close to her and whispered, "What's it taste like?" Her patient, whispered reply was, "Bread." He quietly pondered her answer. Moments later, nudging her elbow and bidding her attention, he further inquired, "Like with butter or plain?" Candid? Genuine? Pure delight!

Surely, another hallmark of young children is their passion for exaggeration. Merely hearing a story is quite insufficient the characters are required to have dramatic voices accompanied, ideally, with realistic sound effects. Exaggeration deeply satisfies children's need to explore limits and to discover possibilities. Their urges to dare and to reveal are satisfied when boundaries are gradually and healthfully pushed back in the learning process. This is why we 'act out' the gospel stories with them, bringing in a fish net, five little loaves and two *real* little fish and provide a mat for the paralytic to lie on and take up when Jesus commands it! All of the drama meets their appetite for the real and for bringing the imagined to life! Therein learning can occur! For, through the human experience, we meet the divine. How clearly children show us this, indeed. (Do expect, though, that they will put their own interpretation on a given story as a fourth-grader did once upon a time, when enacting the miracle of the Wedding at Cana. One of the neighbors preparing to go to the party said, "I don't even know if I'll go. They never have enough wine.") What an irresistible wonder is turned on when costumed characters let go of their self-

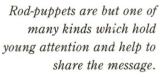

Rod-puppets are but one of many kinds which hold young attention and help to share the message.

consciousness and help the story to happen. Whether in a starring role or bit part, children are inevitably impressed by creative drama and role-playing. Let us use this learning tool to their advantage.

Puppetry of every variation also satisfies the love of exaggeration and characterization. By their wholesome appeal to children's fantasy, puppets can involve children's participation and engagement into a story. Here again, extremes of size can work their charm. Puppets *very large* or very small in size can arrest attention indefinitely, whether manipulated by the cate-chist or children. Try creating some of the stick or handpuppets, or the sock or finger puppets, suggested in a later chapter. Helpful, detailed handbooks on puppet-making are eas-ily available in craft stores to give ideas for both catechists and children.

Surely, one of the delights in working with youngsters is in discovering how literal-minded they are. Call it unsophistication, or innocence, the trait both titillates and startles us in its element of surprise. They "tell it like it is." In inviting a group of third-graders to "pray for the sick of the parish," I was quite tickled at one child's immediate and sincere question, "Why are people sick of the parish?" (Uh-oh.)

One evening, when our family was entertaining a houseguest, I had explained to a then six-year-old daughter that we try to 'see' the Lord in those whom we feed, welcome and serve. Our guest was tired, and began to doze con-tentedly beside the warm fire. The childlike suggestion then, came straight from the pure heart: "Mom, you'd better tell Jesus to go to bed." 'Twas from the mouth of this babe that we heard, also, one day, "Faith is believing in things that aren't true." (Think about it!) Therein is our delightful blessing, if we would but receive it, too. In words as simple as a six-year-old's comment to his Mom about his baby brother who was becoming an eight-month-old delight to him, "Mom, Jason laughs in sentences now." Ah, that we might laugh in sentences more!

The essence of children's transparency is of vital interest to us as creative catechists, in that this quality of their humanness becomes an open gateway to their inner life of faith and their authentic experiences therein. It is their very receptivi-ty to and enthusiasm for *life* which opens them to that *full* life which is their inher-itance and their potential. For this in them we labor with joy as we offer the Truths which they intuit and long to own. Indeed, "the harvest is rich"!

Our young students' natural receptivity and zest press us to create a learn-ing environment conducive to allowing them to sustain interest, involvement and participation in their lesson. Much helpful detail about the faith-learning ambiance will be found in the previous chapter "Setting the Scene: Your Gathering Space." Here, we will emphasize that the learning space should allow as much physical and psychological comfort as possible, provide for those changes of relocation which will support various activities, and generally be a place which (both conspicuously and subliminally) vibrates with life. In a school library where one catechist met with second-graders each week, was a grassy, green carpet in an inviting reading corner. He readily adapted the space as a Judean hillside for relating Gospel stories. How convincing the imaginative space became as the sunshine streamed through the windows and birds sang nearby!

All the more conducive to learning is the classroom in which children's creative activities are prominently displayed to add to the sense of welcome, belonging and hominess.

As catechists, calling forth children's faith, we need to help them to balance their enthusiasm for action and movement with periods of relatively undisturbed quiet, times of productive silence when concentration allows deep thought, and times to simply wonder, to gather and sort out ideas for pondering them. In our conviction that children are, indeed, capable of sustained interior communion, we give them time for moving down through the conscious layers to explore the interior terrain for the enjoyment of the presence of the Spirit. We help them open up to the power – and peace – within, when our time with them includes this balance of inner and outer expression of faith activity.

PROVIDING FOR THE SENSES IN FAITH EDUCATION

In our own sensitivity to the impulsions and characteristics of our young children, as discussed thus far, we become keenly aware that they do look to us in our ministering for those stimulants to learning, those 'vehicles for Truth to ride on,' which meet their hunger for sensory involvement in faith learning. Those promptings suggested here are but a few of the possibilities one could employ. Indeed, let us be creative catechists who never turn down a bit of enticing bait in our "fishing of children." Try these sense activities with your youngsters.

FOR TOUCH

(doing something with the hands, feeling something, expressing with the body):

Use dried, used coffee grounds for roads and fields on a gospel story picture or poster. Brush area with glue, sprinkle grounds on, shake off excess. Feel the realism.

Make an attendance belt. On a large attendance chart made of poster paper, the child attaches a sticker in the square marked off for each lesson on a horizontal row. A dozen lessons seems a comfortable number to sustain interest for this activity with primary children. When all the spaces of each child's line of squares are accounted for with sticker (or a "we missed you" and smiley-face for an absent space,) the child's row is cut off the chart, a hole is punched at each end, yarn is attached to each hole, and the resulting belt is proudly worn home.

Rub a bit of olive oil or baby oil into the skin. Notice its absorption. A powerful aid in lessons on sacraments, gospel stories when oil is mentioned and in discussions on this sign of the Holy Spirit's penetration within ourselves.

Sit and/or kneel on a handmade prayer pillow. Make a 'bag' of sturdy fabric, stuff it comfy, add some owner-designed symbols and pictures to express prayer-time.

Feel popcorn or balloons in their "before" and "after" forms to help children talk about God's gift of ourselves coming into the "more" life at our Baptism. Does not God's breath of the Holy Spirit enlarge us as the human breath swells the balloon? Doesn't the kernel of popcorn become beautiful from the heat a sign of ourselves under the fire of the Holy Spirit?

Make the sign of the cross slowly, calling God by His holy names, dip the fingers into a bowl of holy water for this tiny prayer said with thought and reverence.

Really FEEL gospel props such as rocks, soil, seeds, water, bread, a clay cup, old coins, oil, sheep wool, hay, thorns, rough wood, very large nails, a fish net, real fish, sandals.

Dance creatively or to practiced steps, expressing many moods found in gospel stories: happy, free, sad, frightened, wonder and surprise.

Make music come alive with childmade instruments to rhythmically accompany a cassette or record.

Walk slowly in a procession in the hallway, carrying signs telling Truths learned, wearing biblical costumes, singing a song learned or following a class-made banner.

Break a loaf of bread, share bread and cup of juice during lessons about the Eucharist.

Clap to the rhythm of merry verses and songs; enjoy finger play along with the poems they correlate.

Make and wear a mask made to show particular feelings and unique facial expressions. Might a procession with these delight other classes?

Gather and assemble a collection of interesting seeds identify them and use the collection in prayer appreciating their mystery and life-gift.

Pantomime as a gospel story is being read.

Grind some wheat seed, using two flat stones or a small mill. Use the flour to make some rolls or bread, share the food reverently.

Plant some fast growing seeds, root some cuttings from a branch, plant flowering bulbs. Nurture their growth. Celebrate each sign of life!

Create a simple model of the parish church from a cardboard carton. Make interior furnishings of small boxes and church supply catalog cut-outs; make outdoor shrubbery of crumpled green tissue paper; add a cardboard roof with a bright gold cross fit into a slit at the top.

Create 3-dimensional pictures such as sandpaper deserts, crumpled gray paper rocks, cotton clouds, tiny branch trees and foil paper water. Try the more advanced form of this art in a diorama for enchanting scenes which make stories 'come to life.'

Role play the parts of the Mass, or a Baptism, or the sacrament of Reconciliation, or the Corporal Works of Mercy.

Assemble items and create a Prayer Center a Bible, holy water, a lighted candle, flowers, a simple cloth, a ribbon colored to match the current liturgical season, articles created by children to help express prayer. In the very reverent handling of the articles is great interior value for the child, who subconsciously is previewing the preparation for the larger community's liturgical celebrations.

Offer children, as a sign of welcome, a table at the room's entrance on which are such items as large and small sea shells, colorful stones, moss in a dish of water, various plants, gold fish in a bowl, seeds of all sizes, a bowl of fresh fruit, and (most importantly) a magnifying glass. Post a PLEASE TOUCH sign with the display.

FOR TASTE

(eating foods with a special 'message'):

Heart sandwiches help celebrate Reconciliation.

Cut open and share some fresh fruit, such as a melon, which will reveal numerous seeds; delight in the abundance of God; appreciate God's plan for abundant life even for a fruit!

Chew some wheat seed as background for Eucharist discussions. Rejoice in this universally nutritious food as the staff of life for all.

Cut an apple on its 'equator' to reveal the delightful

surprise in its star-shaped pocket. Enjoy the juicy goodness.

Share heart-shaped sandwiches during lessons on Reconciliation and heart-shaped cookies after the celebration of this sacrament.

Taste a bit of salt, some figs, dates, matzoh (unleavened bread, the kind used in the celebration of Passover). Eat such foods during the hearing of Bible stories' account of their use.

Prepare together and serve the traditional foods of an evening celebration of Passover. Mark Holy Thursday with this meal, drawing out differences and similarities to the Eucharist celebration.

Drink some water reverently and s – l – o – w – l – y, prayerfully appreciate water as the universal sign of life, and its inherent symbolism of full life in Christ.

Prepare and consume several foods made by mixing hot or cold water. Enjoy such activity during lessons on Baptism which can focus on ways which water "makes more" and makes things good, useful and nutritious.

Sample several kinds of bread during a lesson about the Eucharist.

Occasionally enjoy a tasty treat together. When "two or more gather in His name" can be a cause for celebrating with food and for giving children unusual depth to the meaning of Eucharist when food is shared with love.

FOR HEARING

(listening to faith-building sounds):

The catechist's well-modulated voice greeting, teaching, discussing, praying and correcting and dismissing during time with students.

The sound of a child's own name spoken lovingly, and reverently.

The voice of the catechist, whispering when appropriate, compelling attention, and calming.

The chime of one, or several, bells. Try a variety of tones for "moods" that the children suggest,, such as "glorious," "sad" and slow, merry and "calling forth attention." Use bells in music activities for delight.

The prayerful repetition of certain words, such as "Holy, holy, holy," "Come, follow Me," "Glory to God," "I Believe," "Amen, amen." Chant other words from the day's lesson, or from prayers memorized, accompanied with soft, instrumental music in a softly lit room.

The resonance of musical instruments, in reality or on cassette as background while a story is being enjoyed, projects are worked on or during prayertime. Explore the tones of the flute, the harp, soft drums and the piano each for their compelling 'voice.' Make a valuable and sensual accompaniment to stories taking place on the sea, or during storms, or near running water, by playing a cassette of those very sounds. (Such cassettes are available in music shops.)

The listening to a well-told tale… read from the Bible or other appealing book. Hold young audiences captive with varied inflection, expressions, interpretive voicings, description detail and compelling gestures. The shortest distance between the Truth and a child's heart can be often bridged with a story.

The peaceful "sound" of silence during times of reflection, of awareness of God's presence. Balancing an activity with some purposeful silence can be spiritually beneficial.

Hearing the sounds of Nature in quiet, wooded places, in gardens, in vistas where beautiful echoes reverberate.

The subconscious "listening" and being aware of an orderly, secure environment for learning.

The listening to and joining into the singing of children's religious songs, especially when they are relevant to the faithlearning.

Hearing the recorded sounds of the children's voices made during their singing, reading, dramatizing, discussing or praying. How personal the delight becomes during these moments.

Hearing a little bell, to capture the concept of 'conscience.'

FOR SMELLING

(discovering pleasant, or curious, arousing smells, enjoyed with closed eyes.)

Fresh bread; classroom-baked or oven-warm from home. Enjoy during Eucharist lessons or share its goodness just because we are Eucharist people thanking God for such goodness.

Fresh flowers, evergreens or potpourri on a 'welcoming' table or in the prayer center.

Scratch-n-sniff stickers for attendance charts or special papers.

A scented, lighted candle for prayertime.

A bowl of fresh, tangy concord grapes; freshly peeled and sliced oranges, lemons or limes; use any sharply scented fruits which arouse keen appreciation of the varieties in Creation during discussion of same.

Spices and herbs, either fresh or dried, to illustrate those mentioned in Scripture (on which taxes were levied). Use them for appreciating Creation's variety, also.

The special 'treat' of buttered popcorn and hot chocolate when an occasion is celebrated Its message? Perhaps that Friendship and Security 'smell' so good.

Perfume, incense burning, and scented oils help to identify with their Scriptural references to life in Bible times, and use in worship.

An evergreen Advent Wreath or fresh pine tree during the Advent and Christmas season; a manger of fragrant hay at Epiphany.

The fresh air of a well-ventilated classroom.

FOR SEEING

(looking at interesting sights which inspire faith learning):

Symbol of our wholeness and "brokenness," and the restoration back to wholeness within forgiveness

Large, well-lllustrated scenes of Old and New Testament events, tasteful pictures of Jesus, Gospel stories, etc., showing identifiable characters posted at children's eye level and changed occasionally for freshness, interest and classroom visual stimulation.

Numerous photographs or illustrations on a wide variety of subjects. Glean them from magazines, calendars, store displays, posters and the like. Create an enormous picture file at little cost!

Large, well-illustrated picture books of Scripture stories, Nature's wonders, people doing virtuous actions, families of every race and color.

Puppets of all varieties of such is born tremendous visual appeal.

Living vines such as an ivy or grapevine to impress the vine and branches life concept of Christian living.

A lock and key to help in teaching of the 'binding' and 'loosing' of sin in Reconciliation.

Two dishes, one whole, one broken to illustrate wholeness (holiness) and brokenness (sin) in our lives. Use to show what Grace in Reconciliation brings to us: not just glued back together again, but restored to our original wholeness!

A letter of introduction to each child before classes begin in the fall. Include a piece of a jigsaw puzzle, inviting the child to bring the important piece to class on opening day, to be added to the whole puzzle then.

Colorful and huge paper caterpillars and butterflies to emphasize New Life celebrated at our Baptism, and to illustrate our conversion experiences which bring us into the "more" which God promises.

Overhead lights which are dimmed to rest the eyes and relax the spirit; an aid at prayertime, and when entering the room after an outside activity has boosted children's energy.

Colorful signs of "welcome" at the door each bearing a child's name such as a bright leaf, footprint, handprint, smileyface. Post such a greeting for children who join the group during the rest of the year, too.

A large, beribboned helium balloon bearing children's "peace" messages for the finder what a way to raise spirits on Ascension Day!

Scripture verses printed on paper streamers and tacked around the upper walls of the room or going up and down walls and around doorways.

Yeast working in a big glass bowl full of batter. Many Scriptural references will connect with this "slowly, but surely" action.

A moderately large, heavy pumpkin to pass around and guess the number of its seeds an activity to amaze all about God's abundance.

Large, brightly-colored footsteps 'walking' around the room, imprinted with inviting Scripture verses and compelling Christian messages.

A brightly colored hanging-rainbow of God's promises as found in Scripture, each promise written with a sequential color of the rainbow. A stimulating learning activity for the season of Advent.

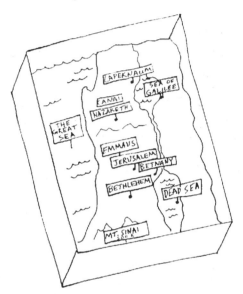

"Something," mysteriously hiding under a cloth, which will later be revealed to the group.

A relief map of Palestine, made of salt-flour clay, showing the terrain, with important locations noted on toothpick supported signs (inserted in place before the map is totally dry); paint appropriately when dry.

Pottery, bowls, cups, jugs, urns made to look old for Biblical scenes. Cover discarded vessels with torn strips of masking tape set on randomly rub the taped surface all over with brown shoe polish, remove the excess for a 'cracked' look use in Gospel dramas.

Large lettered, banner-like visuals expressing the learnings in a given lesson. Use a variety of colors of wide butcher paper, perhaps combining several expressions to give the sense of wholeness, such as in a unit of study a sure-fire room brightener!

Big, brightly wrapped cardboard cartons with Scripture, pictures or Truths being learned imprinted on them; use several as a divider to mark the group's "turf." Make a skyscraper stack of them, too.

A container of rich soil for a child-planted room garden for the growing (and watching!) of easy, fast growing vegetables, wheat and flowers. Correlate this joyful sight to discussions of God's power to make life, God's provision for us.

An ongoing mural of the life of Jesus, including his birth, childhood, His miracles, etc. Or do a mural of the early church as described in the book of Acts or one on living the Sacraments, Beatitudes or Commandments today. Display the creation prominently, signed by all!

A bulletin board of the children's own photographs, perhaps of them doing activities in the room. A real boon to making each student feel like an important part of the whole group. Be sure to include everyone!

Medallions made of salt-flour clay or sturdy tagboard, worn for those special lessons which need extra emphasis to children a small slice of bread imprinted with JESUS IS OUR BREAD OF LIFE, a heart for First Forgiveness lessons, or a large drop of water for learning during the children's catechuminate. (Highly valued: the child imprinting on the symbol.)

Recipe for clay:

> 2 cups flour
> 1 cup salt
> ¾ cup cold water

Mix thoroughly. Form into logs. Wrap with waxed paper. Chill well. Slice with sharp knife. Shape as desired. Bake in low 250°-300° oven, on cookie sheets, 4 hours, turning several times.

A prism perched on a sunny windowsill, or a prism fob dangling in a sunny window. Instant fascination as sunbeams cast bright rainbows all around to remind us of our covenanted God's presence. Try gathering for prayer in a patch of the rainbows!

An exaggeratedly large pair of glasses promoted the message of call to "look with our heart eyes." (Sturdy, colorful poster paper which cuts easily works well for these.)

An enormous pair of eyeglasses with heart-shaped lenses. Make these "eye-catchers" about 3 feet across by 20 inches high complete with hinged ear supports. These exaggeratedly large spectacles become easy focus in discussions about our call to see with love, look for ways to serve, recognizing the Lord in others and whenever children need to recall the Baptism summons to 'see' beyond the earthly life to God's Kingdom.

A roadside sign post, made of a dowel inserted into a stout block, holding two panels made of tagboard; on one panel (a white one for a positive look?) is printed YES, with its arrowpoint to the right. On the other panel (black, of course, to suggest a negative message) is printed NO. The sign post, which should fit on a table top for handy use, is a powerful visual for middle-graders who are revisiting Reconciliation, and need to concretize the concept of free will, that power of choice with which the children of God are graced.

An enormous human ear on which are printed directives for I LISTEN WELL WHEN (for example) 1. I am very quiet, 2. I pay attention with my whole self, 3. I think about what is being said, 4. I remember what I hear. Such simple regulations in the sight of young children will greatly aid them to give their best attention to speakers. Mount the big ear (one about 30″ tall, 24″ wide) onto a background sheet of colorful cardboard larger than the ear, allowing for glued-on pictures of people listening to each other to surround the huge ear.

A moderately large magnet for illustrating the pull of temptations in our life. Children can, with tacks, pins or paper clips, see how people (symbolized by the metallic objects) are drawn into the powerful magnetic field of temptation when allowed by the will to become too close to it. Use this "seeing" to prompt discussion in Reconciliation study about avoiding bad temptations, and likewise, in discussions about the being positively draw toward good temptations, recognizing the magnetic field as Grace being offered. Follow-up activity for such discussion cans include the naming of some good and bad temptations.

Two lengths of clothesline rope, each about 24 inches long. Color, by dipping into tempera or other paint, one rope blue, the other yellow. (The choice of color isn't critical, though they must be two different ones.) To visualize the concept of our union with God, begun at baptism and to continue forever, have the children name one rope GOD the other OURSELF. Ask them how we can show the union which we believe is true?" (The suggestion to "tie them together" will be just about unanimous as their inner vision goes to work here.) Ask the children if God will EVER untie the knot of His love. (They intuit the permanence, bless 'em.) "Might we loosen or untie the knot?" (The consequence of mortal sin is shown in the dramatic untying.) Discuss the "how" of reuniting with God, stressing the deep meanings in true reconciliation examining conscience, recognizing sin, owning the sin, contrition, desiring conversion, confessing, receiving forgiveness, living the promised New Life.
Probe children's thinking and raise their faith consciousness by having them show, with the two ropes, how their union with God will look in the New Life of Heaven. (Intuitively, again, the two ropes will be tied to make a bow or a circle, the ultimate more of the ropes' union!)

A cumulative Gospel story banner/visual to 'see' the collective message of several consecutive Scriptural readings, such as during a Lenten or Advent season. A colorful symbol of each week's message is added on to the large visual which has been entitled with the overall theme of the liturgical season or period.

Realistic 'stone tablets' of the Ten Commandments created from two blocks of Styrofoam (approx. 16″ tall by 14″ wide by 3″ thick). Distress the edges of the blocks by chipping for a more aged look. Print the Ten Commandments in block letters on sturdy art paper and glue them to each tablet. Spraypaint the tablets gray, leaving the printed areas free to remain readable. The large, realistic tablets will lastingly impress young learners who are committing the commandments to memory.

A large basket of colorful vigil lights, each wrapped with a paper band. For a children's communal penance celebration with the theme of "Christ Our Light," place the basket of lights near the parish Paschal Candle in the front of the church; add a small basket of fine-tip felt markers. Invite each child to choose a vigil light, and to write on it (either while in church or later at home) words or symbols which express one's desire and plan for living out the reconciliation experience.

A GOD CALLS MY NAME *banner/visual* to help children imagine the personal speaking of their name by their loving God at their Baptism and henceforth forever. On a sheet of colored butcher paper large enough to accommodate the number of children in the group, imprint Isaiah's prophetic I HAVE CALLED YOU BY NAME. YOU ARE MINE, (43:1). On a sheet of white art paper, the child prints or write his/her name "as lovingly and beautifully as you imagine God speaking it." (Allow time for reflection on this.) Much extravagant color use, design application and pure enjoyment will typify the creation of this visual activity. When one's name is completed, the child cuts out the paper in the shape of a 'cartoon balloon'; they are placed below the Scripture words, collectively conceiving the profound Truth of each one's individual loving proclamation.

A number of balloons, blown up successively more full, and taped in a row on to the blackboard. Above the row is written the question: HOW HAVE I GROWN MORE IN HOLINESS THIS WEEK? Allow for reflection with the children on the desire of the Holy Spirit to make us more and that our cooperation with the Spirit is the infilling of His life-breath. The envisioning will be clearer if all balloons are of the same color; the faith sharing should flow out of the children's consideration of their time of cooperating with the Holy Spirit during the past week.

A family-created banner for the children's celebration of First Communion. Each child/family creates in the home a simple felt banner *of the child's design* which is hung on a pew at First Communion Mass. Uniformity of size might be considered, but much freedom of color, design, words and symbols should be advised. What a glorious SIGHT and faith expression is enjoyed by celebrants when the banners are hung!

In the celebration of Resurrection Day, hide in a familiar setting of shrubbery and grass numerous paper cutout symbols of the Paschal Mystery for children to "hunt and find" and later discuss meanings of them and treasuring for one's own. Include the symbols of wheat, grapes, crown of thorns, the cross, stone tomb, a drop of water, a tongue of fire (the New

Fire,) the Paschal candle, the fish, The Lamb of Victory, the Crown of Christ, three interlocking circles (the Holy Trinity,) the Alpha and Omega (Greek) letters indicating Christ as 'First' and 'Last' of all Creation, and any other symbols which suggest the triumph of Christ.

The writing in lovely script the words I LOVE YOU on a Baptism robe using *indelible* ink to instill deeply the Truth of the everlasting proclamation of these words and their divinely intended meaning.

The video-taping of a typical parish Mass. This invaluable, sense-appealing learning tool will both thrill and educate children. Be sure to capture close -ups of participants as well as the various movements of the liturgy. Begin with the empty church, people greeting one another, etc. and conclude with the empty church which should prompt the query: "Where is the faith community now?" and most importantly, "Where is the Eucharist now?" With youngest children, it is fruitful to show the liturgy in segments and to discuss their details; older students will benefit from seeing the 'whole picture' and will see how the segments move toward the liturgical climax, then proceed toward the dismissal and the redeeming of their world in Christ's name. This becomes a particularly helpful learning aid for children in the catechumenate, as well as those who are preparing for First Eucharist. (Might their parents also greatly benefit?)

A large outline of a church building, cut from a sheet of white art paper becomes a way of visualizing the faith community as the Body of Christ, and the concept that "the church is people, not a building." Onto the blank outline of a church, glue faces cut from magazines and actual photos of the children. Choose those small enough to allow a multitude of them when clustered as a montage. Include people of all races to help visualize the church universal. The overall effect of the church being 'in Christ' can be given by gluing a larger-than-the-church gold halo around it. Mount the living church onto a sheet of colored tagboard and entitle it so that the concept of the visual is well interpreted for your children's level.

The larger-than-life outline of a person can help youngsters conceptualize the Body of Christ when a large picture of Jesus is glued to the outline's head, and smaller pictures of peoples' faces cut from magazines as well as the children's own faces, are glued all over the outline of the Christ figure. Adding photos of people in their family, and others in the parish, will enhance children's interest and deepen the meaning of the overall envisioning of all the baptized as members of the Body of Christ. Be sure to leave blank spaces on the outline for those folks who have not yet become His members!

Inasmuch as this chapter has unfolded for the creative catechist numerous ways in which to enhance children's faith perception through exerting their passion for play and creativity, and exercising their sensory powers, it must be emphasized here that in any given group of students we will encounter several individual styles of learning. Hence, various favored avenues of receiving the message will be awaiting our sensitivity.

These variations call for us to be respectfully aware of those differences in the ways children understand, apply, analyze, synthesize and evaluate what has been intellectually processed. In other words, children receive and 'own' the message through their own individual methods and according to their unique programming mode. Some children direct their learning by hearing the message. Some need to see it quite literally. Still others are more the kinesthetic processors of understanding, and, because all have a right to the message, the Good News, the many styles of learning must be taken into our consideration as their catechists.

Whether, then, their faith learning is achieved through creative imagining, by hands-on experiencing, through one or several sensory channels, or by way of any combination of these powers, we can, and should, provide the environment most conducive to the children's varied learning styles. In this provision, we are not so much "teaching" (pouring in information and facts, or regimenting a particular process or anticipated response) as we are letting a learning environment call forth the child's faith response. We 'listen' with the child, as Maria Montessori wisely counseled. Truly, there is only One Teacher; we are all the listeners.

Our creative catechist role, seen in the light of these considerations about the way our children learn, lies in providing for the creative and sensory paths through which they can become personally and genuinely intimate with their knowledge. Through such paths, the child's inner eye sees what is, truly, best perceived in symbol. Here, Mother Nature is the child's trusted guide. Here, the tangible is made real in the world of the spirit.

This provisional role of ours becomes the highest form of respect and love we can offer to children. This method of teaching becomes the most honest means of passing on faith and of experiencing Truth as we would have it experienced.

In Christ's own words, "The Kingdom of God is within you," our mandate is clear. His Kingdom and very *life* are within our children. We bring it to come in them whenever we walk in faith with them and, therein, celebrate its revelation within them as they receive its blessing.

The first rule
of teaching
is:
"Don't complicate the message."

Anonymous

5

MAKING A GOOD LESSON A GREAT ONE

I enjoy the story about the little fellow whose parents had told him that, since they lived in a busy neighborhood, he was to play only on his own side of the street. Never, they cautioned, was he to cross over to play on the other side. One day the little boy noticed another child about his own age whose family had moved into the house across from his. They began to call to each other, exchanging names and other data pertinent to young children. It was about then that the first little boy said, "I want to play with you, but I can't go across the street." "Neither can I," replied his new friend. "I know, let's meet in the middle!"

Well, here we are, now, surely on ground safer than a busy neighborhood, "in the middle" of these pages, in between discussing the call to being creative people to that of faith teachers who utilize our varied catechetical resources. How appropriate that we should "meet in the middle" now, where the application of our topics will be envisioned in detail. We have been insightful about ourselves as creative, faith-full catechists. We have sharpened our awareness of a faith learning environment. Here, in our lessons with children, everything said as background support will come to life. Here we will put theory and practice together toward making children's learning and faith experiences engaging and fruitful.

"BACK TO BASICS"

As their creative catechist, we will want to be with children right where they are as people developing and journeying in faith. Furthermore, we will want to aid them, through their natural learning avenues, to cooperate with the Holy Spirit in making their faith a living reality. Emphatically, these foundations will support our planning, execution and evaluation of the lessons to ensure that each is consistent with the guidelines given in The National Catechetical Directory. Implicitly, we will want for children to go deeply into their faith place, to take their sensory introductions of faith 'to heart.' Conclusively, we will strive to help children act upon the Truth affirmed simply, to dare to believe. Within these foundations, we will serve our students, in presenting them living faith, as they deserve to be served. Although our procedure for these aspirations will vary somewhat according to our individual teaching styles, these ideals should purposefully guide our efforts. And, in them, we will anticipate the joy which awaits us in our task.

It is toward these ends which the catechist needs to bear in mind that which can be called, primarily, "The Big Picture" of the process of Religious Education. In this larger perspective we see that what is at stake in a child's faith formation is one's incorporating (and gradually incarnating) the following convictions:

(1) that God initiates and desires a viable relationship with the child,
(2) that faith is a gift from God, calling for the child's response,
(3) that Salvation and all of its implicit gifts are offered to the child through Jesus Christ, and
(4) that power within the child for living out the message of the Gospel is the promised gift of the Holy Spirit.

It is out of this framework that the child will learn to give living testimony and self-expression to the tenets of one's faith. It is within this larger structure of Truth that he/she will enjoy the freedom of full and fruitful living. Clearly, as their catechist, we are but a guiding instrument, steadying the course of the exciting journey of faith. A tremendous privilege, indeed, is given to us!

IN THE BEGINNING

It is in the light of this Big Picture and its application, that we aptly question "When, where and how might a great lesson begin?" Might it begin in a prayerful moment before the class gathers? In a few days before, with paper, pencils and textbook handy at the kitchen table? On a relaxing walk, when you are inspired with a terrific idea? In the market, where you see a particular advertisement that "fits" the lesson? Perhaps its beginning might be at a liturgy, when you hold up your students to the Lord. Or might a great lesson begin with your own "Yes," as you are called and commissioned as a catechist in the Christian community? Broadly speaking, might the genesis of a great lesson come from somewhere deep within the womb of the heart, where we have come to faith as Christ's disciple?

Our answers, surely, lie within each and all of these possibilities. Our lessons, though perhaps outlined by another, such as a text's authors, do need to be born from within, "hatched in the heart" as reflections of our very selves as a faithfull, worshipping, organized, enthusiastic and creative catechist. Furthermore, I contend that the Truth which we are called to prophesy as participants in the continual renewal of the whole Church, will be most efficaciously transmitted by the catechist whose life is one of holiness, of consecration to the will of God. It is within this standard that we, Christ's instrument, are in tune with the very message we offer others. Our witness to the Truth must, necessarily, go before us.

AND OUT OF THE SOURCE

Let us be clear about this emphasis on the holiness of the catechist, for upon this foundation will surely rest the validity of our personal witness to the Truths of our faith. Scripture makes it clear that, through Christ, God's people are to be holy, just like God is (1 Peter 1:15-16). Christ loved the Church and gave himself up for her precisely to make her holy (Eph. 5:25-26). Union with Christ not only expects our holiness but produces it in greater degree. Such union fulfills God's will for us the holy way of life (1 Thess. 4:3; Eph. 1:4). Vatican II teaches that the call to holiness is for everyone – for the whole Church (Lumen Gentium, 39). This call to holiness is especially important for catechists! We must first and foremost be a recipient of and a participant in that grace and action of the Holy Spirit before catechesis can be authentic and effective! There is little power of God's life shining through us if all we have to offer is correct (that is, orthodox) knowledge. The prophetic power of catechesis is significantly decreased when there is little real and personal appropriation of the divine life of holiness within the catechist. Conversely, a holy life radiates, illuminates and substantiates the message one is offering.

Out of what, then, must our great lesson be draw up? Verily, from the fount of Truth in the center of our being! From here flows the promised "living water" (John 7:38) for our children's thirst. That which is received and loved within the catechist, then, will be freely given to others, so that the gift of faith might live on. And in this perpetuating is our very great joy.

THE "CATECHIST'S EYE VIEW" OF THE LESSON

Never can the value of thoroughly planning a lesson be underestimated. Expending time and energy on all the necessary considerations for it will reap immeasurable reward for you and your learners. Part of our previous focus on the four "Big C's" focused on the thoroughness of our preparation for effective teaching to occur. Simply stated, there is no substitute for the organizing of the lesson's time, for systematically arranging for each movement of the procedure and for thinking through the possibilities, and probabilities, of the various elements within the whole process.

One of my planning helps is in visualizing well beforehand the moments of a lesson, and in imagining the children's likely responses to questions or discussion points. It's impossible, of course, to predict accurately what will 'happen' when children are involved. And rare is the occasion when, from our welcoming to the reaching our final goal, we enjoy a smooth flow just as we have planned it. Yet, our mental envisioning of the lesson's progress will support our planning for it as realistically as possible.

Foremost in our thorough planning should be several overall considerations. Our overviewing of a given lesson will proceed with certain questions which will serve well in our later evaluating, also; (that marvelous 20/20 hindsight which is critical to marking progress). Thus, our lesson planning should include responses to these concerns.

a. What Truth will I be presenting to the children in this lesson?

b. How will I be presenting this Truth, in order to meet their various needs?

c. What procedure will I follow to advance the lesson, from initially honoring the child's experience of the subject, to the child's comprehending of the Truth and assimilating it meaningfully into one's life?

d. What visual, auditory and tactile aids will be employed throughout the lesson to promote interest, participation and understanding of the Truth? From where will these resources be available?

e. What creative involvement will help the children to personalize and interiorize the Truth of the lesson? What resources will the creative activities require in preparation?

Herein, through answering such concerns in a detailed outlining of the lesson, will rest our expectations for touching each child and eliciting one's faith response. It is essential for us to cast this "catechist's eye view" upon our lesson plan, in order to organize its timeframe and to reach its objectives successfully.

LIKENING LESSON PLANNING TO MEAL PLANNING

There is a profound similarity in preparing for a lesson and preparing for a nourishing meal. Comparing them is helpful and enables a certain comfortable procedure to direct us as creative catechists who, wholeheartedly, want to 'feed' our children well. Note the similarity of the two processes, and let them help in your planning.

First, and foremost, in planning for either a lesson or a meal, *we must have a sincere desire to nourish our people.* We need to offer the best quality and contents we possibly can, so that those who partake will ultimately be healthier for having "eaten at our table."

We make detailed plans for the togetherness time. From welcoming others to making them comfortable conversationally, and into the partaking time, we anticipate others' needs and think through ways in which we might try to meet them. Essentially, we plan for the food (which, in our task, is for the whole Truth) to be attractively offered and stimulatingly presented, bearing in mind that "we eat first with the senses." So, our setting and our menu will receive our deepest consideration.

We acquire the ingredients. It should be a joyous search, for our cause is so very noble in either endeavor. This will ask our being resourceful, and at times ingenious, with our talents, abilities and budget. Some of the ingredients will be "home made." Some perhaps will be borrowed. Others acquired from our well of experience and creativity. All the ingredients will contribute meaningfully to the whole "meal" and toward the aim of nourishment.

We decide how we will offer the "food." There will be gradual courses, each taking its time for savoring. There will be various "appetites" to satisfy. The "meal" will progress slowly, purposefully, giving time for the assimilating of each portion. Each step will flow smoothly and sensibly into the next. There will be an overall sense of enjoyment of the occasion.

We add a few sheer delights. Garnishes enhance the dishes of food. A few surprises will color our presentation and stimulate pleasure in the eating. It is the unexpected 'touch' which so often becomes a lasting memory after a wholesome meal. Interest is piqued when children are amazed, surprised and pleasantly caught off guard during learning.

We are ever mindful of the partakers' lasting benefits. Enjoyment and companionship, although important to it, are not the heart of the meal. Surely, only nourishing food will lastingly benefit the eaters. Foremost in our design is the sending of people on their way truly fed, genuinely provided for and strengthened for the journey ahead. This is what matters after all the "dishes" are cleared away. Soul and body will have benefited. Healthy digestion and being energized are our major precedences when we are true to our vocation as "a good cook," both in the kitchen and in the children's classroom.

In this language of comparisons can be seen those areas which need to be accentuated in lesson planning, so that, after all, there is the vitalizing and renewing of faith within the child at every partaking of the Truth. And, realistically, just as the appetite for more substantial food increases with our natural development, so does childrens' need for truly invigorating presentations expand with maturity. Our challenge is to prepare for every step in satisfying and honoring their God-given hunger for Truth. There is every reason, then, for thorough preparation for the time we will spend in opening up children to their gift of faith. Our respect for them, and our desire to help them develop, will ask this of us. Simply, achievement of every kind will depend upon our foreseeing, to the greatest possible degree, all of a lesson's potential efficacy.

If children need from us our in-depth preconception of their lessons, they just as critically need within themselves a sense of purpose in their coming to learn. Children bring to our time together a simple, most often unarticulated, question: "What should be happening here?" It is an inquiry full of expectation on their part, and one which deserves honoring, as we, in our sensitivity, present them early on with clear expectations of behavior, manners, objectives and responsibilities for everyone. These issues may be addressed by our printing, for example, acceptable listening standards on an enormous, realistically drawn ear. We might respond to their wonderful question by showing an extended sequence of lessons' titles listed on a horizontal strip of paper posted in the room, complete with dates and clever pictures to illustrate them. Such a visual aid will help children to relate one lesson to the scope of a whole unit, the better to chart their own progress in learning. (Surely, we all like to know what we can expect will be happening over a period of time, and that seeing it "in print" gives one a sense of connecting to what we're involved in at a given time. This is evermore helpful for young children.) Giving children explicit directions, full explanations of rules and 'limits' and insisting on mutual respect will create an atmosphere where fairness, order and consistency will prevail. We respond to childrens' unspoken prerequisite for learning by offering them the highest quality of environment in which it can occur.

"FEED MY LAMBS"

Rarely do hungry youngsters need to be called to a good meal more than once. We're quite familiar with their healthy appetites. We are well aware of their need for lots of nutrition on their plate. And, as has been stressed, the child's hungers in the natural world interestingly correlate to the growing need for a well-balanced diet of Truth in order to develop spiritually. So, we will return to the similarity of our lesson being very much like a well-prepared meal for them. (Perhaps Jesus meant for us catechists to interpret somewhat literally the charge to "Feed My Lambs." We will let it be a reliable guide for us in our shaping "great lessons.")

THE THREE STEPS IN OUR LEARNING-TIME "MEAL"

Three fundamental movements will flow together within a great lesson.

(1) The appetite for involvement is stimulated.
(2) The food of Truth is presented and ingested.
(3) The digestion of faith-full response, the being energized, occurs.
     We will look closely, now, at how these steps apply to our faith lessons.

Movement 1 relates to the children's appetite being aroused for the lesson's Truth. We have gathered together, have been welcomed and personally recognized. We are comfortable in an environment which is both stimulating and oriented to faith. This beginning-time of the lesson should draw the child in physically, socially, mentally and emotionally. Within this comfort zone, one will allow the good ground of the spirit to become open to the imminent sowing of the seeds of Truth. Only attentiveness and participation will flow from the hospitality/orientation in the opening moments of a lesson. How critical, then, is our awareness of their initial responsiveness. (I do not hesitate to invoke the power of the Holy Spirit upon the children during this gathering time, and to pray for the casting out, in Jesus' name, all influence of the enemy. I ask for the infusion of the Spirit's gifts upon each child. This orders my heart, and puts the whole of what will follow in the Lord's hands, and relieves me of the feeling that the lesson will depend entirely upon my limited resources.)

During this time, there is purposefully some "thinking about," "sharing from your life" and discussion/dialogue about the subject of the lesson. We encourage each child to offer ideas, being especially sensitive to the reticent ones, as well as to those who might tend to dominate conversation. Hopefully, all are able to contribute in a valuable way when we are receptive and tactful during this movement.

It is helpful to be aware that primary-age children tend to relate a given topic almost exclusively to themselves, to their lives. To them, it is important that something "happened to me," that they personalize the experience under discussion. Their concepts at this age are formed and driven by their own review of the matter. As children mature, they are more able to perceive an idea from another's perspective, more abstractly, a development which calls forth our respectful recognition of quite a variety of opinions and viewpoints when a class of middle or upper-graders is our particular 'vineyard.' The primary child generally is limited in life-experience, and builds upon what is already known and experienced. I was delighted to witness this trait of very young children when, just as he was leaving home for another busy day in kindergarten, and we were pausing to have a little prayer, my son said, "Pray for me, Mom, I'm line leader today." Indeed, they pronounce faith "right where they are." (And I was glad he knew where good line leaders get their power!)

A variety of visual, auditory and tactile aids will contribute to interest and participation during this arousal of appetite step. Some will help to introduce the topic. Others will engage the children in conversation. How essential for them to focus their senses upon the topic in a tangible way, the better to track, or follow, what is being presented to them. So, pictures, a story dramatized, a short film, an audio tape, a hand-held object all serve in this appetite-arousal step.

We will look, now, at a typical lesson to see how this beginning movement can open up children to their lived experiences. We will observe the value which its components can have for the learners. In this sample lesson, the planned Truth to be presented is We Offer Our Gifts To God at Mass. The catechist is helping children who are preparing for their First Holy Communion. The period of time is 1¼ hours long.

Their 'meal' begins as the children are seated, following some initial welcoming and hospitality. They are seated in horizontal rows of chairs, simulating the setting of their church, complete with an aisle in the center of the arrangement. Their learning environment includes an altar/table in the center-front of the rows, a gift table at the rear on which are lighted candles, a dish of flat, round crackers and a small, glass pitcher of fruit juice, both simulating the ritual gifts of bread and wine. The parish family book, in which are written the names of people they wish to pray for, also awaits on the table. Realism prevails. Interest is motivated.

The learning environment also includes a large paper banner in the front of the room. On it are a number of ripe wheat stalks which are 'bending over' a dish of communion breads. Adjacent to the graphically portrayed wheat and bread is a large bunch of paper grapes shown 'pouring into' a chalice of wine. The visual message of our gifts to God at Mass shows them giving themselves to become something more. On a side table are a large real sheaf of wheat and a juicy bunch of real grapes, providing further emphasis of the lesson's message. A crucifix is hung near the banner to complete the essence of this part of the Mass being presented in the lesson.

"WHETTING THE APPETITE"

A large box introduces the topic of gift-giving. Its Disney motif wrapping paper and bright bow prompt quick pondering of its possible contents. Discussion of the delights in receiving and giving gifts progresses. Experiences are eagerly shared of gifttimes in their families and friendships. Certain feelings about gift experiences are mentioned. Imagination and wonder come into the sharing as do guesses of what might be in such a large gift which is passed now among the children, and shaken for 'clues.' Soon another gift, a small, wrapped box is presented for discussion. What might be in it? To whom might one give such a tiny gift? On what occasion? Have they ever seen this done? We speak of the two different sizes of the gifts, considering whether "bigger is automatically better." Their insights are now quite keen in thinking through the value of either as a possible gift.

Sometimes children perceive that to be really a gift, the item must have been purchased, for often such has been their experience. Yet in our desire to move them ever more deeply into Truth now, we focus on the value in *making* gifts and they tell of their experiences of such. Examples are cited, suggestions are offered. When they are shown a small, clay vessel given to the catechist by her (now adult) child many years ago, they discuss why one would keep such a gift. Insight leads them to telling that certain memory of the giver remains within the gift surely an intuited and applicable understanding of the gift of the Eucharist which will gradually come to light. Someone mentions that the great thing about giving handmade gifts is that one can "put a lot of love in it." The whole value in giftgiving which seems to surface is that, whether it is purchased or made, it is necessary that the giver somehow participate in the giving, another graced reference to Eucharist moments, certainly.

Now, ready to go ever deeper into the discussion, we ponder invisible gifts something "hidden" inside such as love, good wishes, forgiveness, friendship. Might such a gift be offered in a particular gesture? In one's body language? In certain actions? Now for more inner searching of experiences. Yes, the work our parents do for us, the smiles from a teacher, a hug from a parent – insights attesting to experiences of giving to another on a heart-to-heart level. We talk of the value of such a gift what might we be 'saying' with it? What will make such a gift mean so much? We dramatize such gift-giving to emphasize their meanings. Some comment on how difficult it might be to give, or to receive, a gesture, because "you have to mean what you are giving." This enables them to intuit that the expression conveys one's gift, and that the message of love, forgiveness, etc. must necessarily come from one's heart for it to be real. Thus, they have been led to look deeply within such a gesture (or invisible) gift for what the expression if it means.

(Creative catechist, now we are reminded of Jesus' style of teaching, His use of tangible expressions to illustrate a "hidden Truth." "What comparison shall we use for the reign of God? What image will help to present it?" (Mark 4:30) A few loaves and fish concealing a mystery of the ultimate Eucharist banquet, a vine and its branches, a drink of water at a well, bread broken, a cup shared with friends – all cloaked a secret, leading the participants deeply into its home, the heart. When we move with children from the tangible to that which awaits within to be known we are, indeed, doing as He did. Let His example of bringing people into their interior faith place, and letting the heart claim what has been illuminated, be our guide in our catechizing of children.)

This engaging step in our lessons becomes a veritable 'gateway,' leading into the lesson's heart of Truth. We have drawn upon their experiences. They have considered, and have contributed to one another's understanding. Objects have prompted keen interest. The children feel that their presence and thoughts are valuable. They anticipate "more," that the procedure thus far will, somehow, lead to continuing involvement. Indeed, it will, for the appetite has been aroused, the 'food' of Truth will be put before them as the next logical step in the 'meal.'

AND JESUS SAID TO THEM, "COME AND EAT"

Continuing with likening of a lesson to a nourishing meal, we see how naturally this central segment of it flows from the previous discussion and how assuredly it will offer the children some Truth to own. As always, it is important for young children to sensualize and concretize that which is abstract and mysterious. Objects, then, will now connect them to Truth. More to the point, the Truth will come to them, as they are actively and sensually engaged and open to its revelation. Faith's work will continue. Seeing will, providentially, lead to believing. We are there to help it happen, simply and naturally, for them.

SERVING THE "FOOD THAT ENDURES"

During these prime time moments, the catechist wonders, with the children, what gifts we might offer to God when we are at Mass. What might our bread and wine "say" to God for us? What might we each give which is included in the offering – something invisible? They are led to the Truth that we each might give *something which God doesn't have until we offer it:* ourselves, our love, our heart. Long moments of quiet thought now help this Truth to settle within each child's faith place. Later, when at Mass, they will listen carefully to the priest's words as he speaks for all of us. He will affirm their faith that our perfect gift to God, His Son Jesus, is offered along with our selves, our love and our lives. Although the divine exchange of our gifts becoming the Body and Blood of Jesus will remain a deep mystery for them, the impression remains meaningful that our gifts at Mass are offered in love with full heart and sincerity.

Here, their understanding begins of what the symbolic gifts of bread and wine mean, what they "say" for us as they are offered: "We praise you, God," "We give you Jesus, our best gift," "I love you, God." Thus, the child is making a meaningful connection between symbolic action and his own interior life, and can better enter into these moments, personalizing them with heartfelt involvement. All of this focus upon our "giving our gifts to God at Mass" lesson is, of course, presented to children in simple, understandable language and with repeated explanation, including the dialogue and gestures appropriate to this part of the Mass. Time is necessarily given for questions, observations and clarifications as needed. Visual and auditory perception is keen, as objects and words aid the message. In this central part of any lesson, we are concerned with leading the child as deeply as possible into one's faith place within, in order to give time for responding personally, unique ly and genuinely to the food of Truth being 'ingested.' Therein, is the 'eating' occurring in their learning 'meal.'

"AND THEY ALL ATE AS MUCH AS THEY WANTED"

The children's attention is drawn to the large wheat/grapes visual as we talk of the two symbols and of what they mean for us at Mass. They tell what they know about wheat as it develops and grows, having planted and nurtured some wheat seed prior to this lesson, a valuable hands-on experience now recalled as a pot of healthy wheat grows on a nearby windowsill.

Wheat's gift of itself in becoming our bread is appreciated, with particular mention of its presence in our altar bread. In the same way, the grapes on the visual will be revered for their gift to us as our communion wine. Sensitively, the catechist will lead them to recognize that it is in the dying and rising up to new life which the two elements have let happen that we can better understand Jesus' resurrection the "more" life, as we choose to call it. (Take advantage of such teachable moments and their opportunities to lead children deeply within). Now the learners pass around and admire a sheaf of real wheat and a juicy bunch of grapes on a dish to intensify the impact of their becoming inner life for us at Eucharist.

FURTHERING THE TRUTH WITH ROLE-PLAYING

With the children imagining that they are now at Mass, the role-playing of the offering of our gifts becomes a dynamic vehicle for the Truth to 'ride on.' A

The power in role-playing becomes an influential learning tool for primary children

child-priest is ready at the little altar/table; he wears a chasuble to identify his role as presider. Gift-bearers await at the rear for their presentation procession, reverently holding the dish of 'breads,' pitcher of 'wine' and family book of names. Ushers are taking up the collection of envelope gifts (handed out to the children previously, having been donated by the parish bookkeeper). Altar servers have placed the priest's chalice on the altar. Attention to these preparatory moments is thoughtful and keen. The procession of gifts begins.

Having received the gifts, the 'priest' leads the prayers of blessing over them, reading from a placard on the altar. "Blessed are you, Lord God of all creation, in your goodness we have this bread to offer." He holds the dish during the prayer and during the response, "Blessed be God forever!" Prompting cards, in the shape of large cartoon/balloons imprinted with the responses, guide the children during these moments, adding to the comfort level of participation. During this role-playing, the progression of this part of the Mass, i.e. our lesson, is slow, deliberate and relaxed. The children and catechist comment on what is happening in order to enhance the learning. The students are alert to the opportunity for offering their love, thanks and praise together with the bread and wine. The solemnity of these moments is sustained as the child opens up one's heart to the action and affirms one's own moments of gift-iving.

Do children sense the sacred, we might ask? Indeed, they not only perceive it, but are drawn to participating in its mystery! I have, at times, seriously desired to reach the depth of devotion which I have witnessed in children at worship. They have much to teach us by their simple and sincere expressions of faith.

Through their uninhibited role-playing here, of a sacred ritual, young children not only become more familiar with the movements and dialogue within it, they are more compelled to enter into what is unfolding, having seen, heard and touched its elements. How naturally their senses have, once gain, served them as the learning vehicles which they are.

"WITH EARS TO HEAR"

At the time of the proclamation of the "Holy, holy, holy . . ." prayer, the catechist directs the children to "listen for the unity," for our "one voice" in it. Everyone is contributing to the one voice of the community gathered here, just as at Mass when, in unity, we call out to the Lord, in unity we want to come to the Lord, in unity we want Him to come to our parish, so that in that unity we will respond to people's needs as Jesus did. Hearing (again, the power of the senses!) the unison in this prayer impresses upon them our belonging to each other, perhaps a newly discovered concept regarding their worship.

Reviewing what takes place in the heart of this sample lesson, the creative catechist will see the high level of children's participation throughout. One will note the visual and tactile tools which aide in their connecting attentively to the Truth presented. Having arrived at a meaningful level of understanding, they are able to move easily from sharing personal experiences of gift-giving to the deeper degree of self-giving within the context of worship at Eucharist. The food of Truth is presented attractively, the menu is appealing to the diverse group of youngsters, which respect to their age levels and backgrounds of familiarity in attending Mass. As the children's catechist helps them to appreciate the Truth which they have begun to call forth from within, he/she will enjoy marveling with them that we are a church which celebrates giving our gifts to God and recognizing with them that each individual's offering, in union with Jesus, is important.

"WHO HAS A QUESTION?"

In our concern for helping them to process learning, we will also be keenly aware of the dynamics in asking questions related to the subject at hand. What power there is in a well phrased question!

To foster children's faith learning, we will try to ask those questions which presume the 'answer' is within the child, within the dialogue he/she has with the Spirit. Questions such as the following might be most productive, since they invite some interior movement and reflection from the hearer:

"Why do you think Jesus said (or did) that?"

"What would happen if. . . ?"

"What do you think it would be like to . . . ?"

"What was Jesus (or the man, woman, child, etc.) feeling in their heart when . . . ?"

"What do you think you would say if Jesus asked you to . . . ?"

"What did you hope would happen in the story?"

"Why would you feel this way?"

We will also draw questions *from* the children, concerns which reveal their probing, and considering of a matter. Within the teaching dynamic of questioning lies the vast potential for growth in the Spirit, a joy for both catechist and learners.

SAVORING THE FOOD OF TRUTH

The third 'course' in a great faith lesson is typically much loved by both catechist and children. Comes now the digesting and being energized by the nourishing Truth. Herein, we are concerned with the child's understanding of what has been presented, and in one's affirming and validating the learning in an expression of personal, meaningful and living faith within the newfound Truth. There is a child's natural desire, now, to express what has been "learned by heart." We help them to honor this need to communicate in a unique way what the heart has begun to own. In these moments, the child will be true to oneself, for what will be declared will have sprung from one's own graced being. What delight we can look forward to as the presented Truth is echoed and reflected, just as tiny rainbows are revealed in a sunlit prism. How sacred are these moments in the lesson, as the work of the Spirit is revealed within the child.

The 'savoring' during these moments is much like that which occurs when, after a delicious meal, participants sit around the table digesting food and letting the nutrition do its unhurried work. Surely, it is one of the most beneficial contributions to overall health. And, just so will this interval of creative activity be for our young learners. There will be deep satisfaction, now, as we witness children sharing ideas and expressing them creatively in a personalized and enjoyable way. Let this pleasure be an indicator for the catechist, who plans thoughtfully and resourcefully for this quality time in the faith lesson.

Our frame of mind concerning the creative expression at this time should not be for the child to try for perfection, nor for the production of something pre-ordained by the teacher. We will simply, *in our full respect for the child's integrity,* provide the means for the expression of Truth; we will offer material for the announcing of the Truth with which they are now beginning to be at home.

During this movement in our sample lesson, the children are aware that the culmination of these several gatherings will be their First Communion liturgy. The catechist guides their discussion of the presentation of altar gifts at their coming liturgy. She interests the children in planning a way for them each to participate actively in the special moments by each creating a love message to God on a hand-sized, tri-folded heart.

The practicalities of presenting the heart messages are discussed; the issue is voted upon to decide whether to put all the hearts into a prettily decorated basket to be carried forward by one or two children, or to connect all the heart messages with colorful yarn to form a chain which several students might present at their offertory. Thus, the catechist encourages the children to imagine, and "see with your heart eyes" this part of their liturgy, allowing them to not only use their decision-making skills, but to invest something of themselves in a meaningful way into the procedure and decision.

After settling on the option of the chain of hearts, they answer enthusiastically the question of what message might be drawn or written on one's heart. Again, as a review, messages of thanks, praise and love are accentuated. These moments of preparation for their creative activity become a marvelous opportunity for all to reaffirm their participation in the gift presentation at every Mass. They confirm anew that our gifts of bread and wine speak for our hearts in that they are God's gifts to us out of the earth which, at Mass, hold everything we should say to God. So, pictures of these bread and wine symbols are included in the suggestions. (I have found that since children at this young age are just beginning to be introduced to the mystery of the crucifixion and its centrality for the believer at Eucharist, they might refer to Jesus' death on the cross more as something which happened historically, rather than as a event that is memorialized as occurring at every Eucharistic offering, a concept which will be broadened in their maturity. Yet, they intuit its rightful presence at our worship. Therefore, they include pictures of the crucifixion and often the resurrection in their suggestions for decorating their heart messages.)

HEAD, HEART AND HANDS TOGETHER IN FAITH

Again, the young children have an opportunity to vary their postures as now they stand at tables which have been "set" with their pastel hearts, crayons, and felt tip markers. Each is enjoying the freedom of choosing what will be inscribed and drawn, and in selecting the art media for doing so. Some visit together to share ideas. Some are soon quietly engrossed in the activity, confident of their effort at the start. A few need prompting or confirming of ideas before beginning. All are ready to make concrete that which the heart knows crystallizing it in its finest sense. The catechist seems to sense the hovering of the Spirit over the children, as inspiration, creativity and delight pervade the room. It is a time to allow the Spirit's movement within each person, as the young heart confides what it believes.

As each completes a heart message, having inscribed and symbolically decorated it, the young artist seals its two front halves closed with one of a selection of stickers bearing Jesus' picture. They then delight in forming their heart chain on the rainbow-colored yarn, and in holding it high as it will be held in their offertory procession. Someone suggests attaching flowers and colored ribbon to the chain. Others offer to help with this. This step of digesting continues, as members are selected to bring forward the gift chain at this Mass. Each child will have been intimately involved in bringing to the fullness the creative expression of "giving our gifts to God at Mass."

Because effective catechesis is the gradual unfolding of the Truth within the hearer, it follows that the ultimate fullness of this lesson's creative expression will truly be known at the children's First Communion Mass for which they are preparing and in continuum at every Mass in which they will subsequently participate. Such is the way and life of the Spirit at work in the good ground of faith. We simply assist toward the promised fulfillment of the young sprouting seed.

Seated now, in a circle, the children will gather around the chain, enjoying the song, A Gift From Your Children (Carey Landry and Carol Jean Kinghorn, *Hi God* 3). As they listen to the words on the cassette singing of the very Truths of their lesson, and as they join in with the chorus, they again affirm knowingly the giving of their gifts to God, as well as the words of the very song they are singing. Here, now, there is both quiet, active listening, singing, and proffering of their belief that God loves their offerings of hand-works, thoughts, love, bread and wine, and Jesus, our Savior. The song wraps up for the participants, as neatly as a gift package, the understandings they have learned, and confirms for them the Truth now so alive in their hearts.

THE "GREAT" POTENTIALITY IN EVERY LESSON

In following the detailed movements of the above sample lesson, the creative catechist will see how closely a faith lesson can resemble a well ordered meal, and will let this principle work to the children's learning advantage. Young children need to be fed the learning in tantalizing bites, tasting each as they move through its courses. I enjoy applying the analogy because of its reliability in honestly working toward its purpose: the healthy nourishing of Truth. This basic meal/lesson precept can be easily applied to any faith lesson, with the details of each movement made unique to each theme. The outline seems an uncomplicated tool for one's planning, execution and evaluation purposes. Let it serve to magnify the quality of a "good lesson" (which often needs just more the catechist's sensitivity,) so that its participants will experience a truly great lesson.

What is at stake in our presenting children a high quality faith lesson is basically a two fold projection: (1) the child's journeying into the spiritual realities of this present life and (2) the child's potential commitment to living out those realities. Out of these potentialities, let every faith lesson reach deeply into the child's ability to live faith, to believe in the indwelling Savior Christ, and to call upon the love and power of God in one's everyday walk. Great lessons help a child's heart to discover and know that God waits to be conceived, wants to be believed and longs to be received. Such criteria will move a good lesson into one which is truly "great."

CHOOSING THE CREATIVE ACTIVITY WISELY

The step of engaging children in a creative expression of what they have learned is, rightly so, of much concern to the catechist. In these moments, the child will reveal the response to the Truth which the heart has received. Surely, we want for the revelation to be genuine and sincere, as well as an apt expression of faith now owned. Far from this being simply an arts and crafts time, this segment of our lessons is meant to help one to give some crystallizing and concretizing to the Truth within. As creative catechist, we value this expression as the digesting of the food of Truth received. Therefore, what is expressed deserves to meet certain criteria for judging its value as a creativity in our religious education planning. Offered here are four areas of judgment for considering an activity's use in a faith lesson (The following headings are adapted, in part, from *Classroom Creativity* by Elizabeth Jeep; Herder and Herder, 1970).

The idea should be theologically sound. It should express some essential Truth of our faith. The song, art activity, drama or other expression should point to a Truth the student is learning. It should help the child grow in awareness of, and love for, God, self and all others. It should develop awareness of the Catholic doctrines and traditions for the child.

The idea should be educationally valuable. Repetition and review should be employed as valuable to learning. To further the learning process:

The activity should demand some creative effort, mental energy and physical involvement, all to the child's maximum ability within the constraints of time.

The activity should deepen the child's understanding of a Truth, building continually upon what is already learned. (For example, after having written a list of many gifts God gives to us, the faith learning deepens when the child draws or paints a picture of herself enjoying a specific gift, personalizing the revelation all the more.

The activity should be the personal expression of the child and not the endorsement of another; nor need it be directed toward pleasing the adults. The activity should show all that the child can bring to it. (For example, adding a short prayer to a drawn picture, then using both in a para-liturgy or giving the activity as a gift or adding a frame and displaying. A learned song might be sung for a small audience, clapped to or included in a prayer.)

The idea should be artistically stimulating. This implies respect for some freedom within the child. Drawings might naturally show distorted shapes and unrealistic proportions. (Do I cherish the picture drawn of Noah's Ark flying an American flag?) Yet, whether the expression is through the creative arts, the dramatic arts or the visual arts, it is through and in the inner artistic freedom of the child that the Truth becomes a part of one. The creative expression becomes artistically stimulating when children are helped.

to understand the 'value' of colors warms, colds, intensities, etc.
to compose a drawing or writing, working out ideas from a central one.
to research a character being portrayed dramatically.
to explore a variety of creative media for expressing learning and the varied forms within the given media (poetry and prose in writing, mime and recitation in drama, etc.).
to indulge their natural affinity for exaggeration and repetition.
to attempt untried artistic skills, overcoming inhibitions and a natural resistance to "new" methods of expression.
to, above all, understand the purpose of the activity and its relevance to the Truth it expresses.

Further criteria for judging the value of an activity which expresses faith learning:

The activity is appropriate for the given age group.
The activity has not been already over used so as to become tiresome.
All materials for the activity are, or can be, readily acquired.
The activity can be completed in a reasonable length of time.
The students are sufficiently motivated, by a story, discussion, music, pictures, etc., toward expressing learning with an activity. Sufficient stimulation for keeping children interested in the progressive unfolding of the Truth has occurred.
The students feel sufficiently capable and confident of making a meaningful contribution if the activity is a group endeavor, such as a mural, a dramatic presentation or a para-liturgy.

CREATIVE ACTIVITIES WHICH HELP CHILDREN INTERIORIZE FAITH

It would be difficult to list here all the benefits to children's faith formation from their involvement in creative activities. Each of the 'courses' of their lesson/meal might easily incorporate one or several means for creative expression by either catechist or child, as we have recommended in our sample lesson.

The following suggested activities are given to help catechists select creative possibilities which can "give life" to each of the segments of the lesson, therein helping children to encounter and express faith learning. Included is a general explanation of the medium, and suggestions for specific activities within each category.

For convenience, the suggestions are presented in three separate categories: The Performing Arts, The Visual Arts of 2-dimensional quality, and The Visual Arts having a 3-dimensional quality. (This form of categorizing of the suggestions was adapted from *Classroom Creativity* by Elizabeth Jeep, Herder and

Herder, 1970.)

I. The Performing Arts

Music

The extensive used of records and tapes for background mood conducive to carrying on other creative activities, the playing of instruments to accompany singing, the learning of some 'singable' songs, including those appropriate to the liturgical seasons the composing of songs by individuals or a group to express learning and to become part of a prayer.

Gesture

The 'talking with our bodies,' the physical expressing of a song, prayer, gospel text, the acting out of what is being listened to, the awareness of our use of gestures in our relationships and at Eucharist such as a bow, handshake, hug, nod, opening of arms in prayer, the offering of a gift. Enjoy the "Our Father" with gestures; include discussion of the negative speaking we sometimes do with our body language.

Dance

The free interpretation of feeling expressed during or following the hearing of a gospel story, a particular incident or a piece of prose or poetry related to the lesson, possibilities for interpretive dance include the "calming of the storm," the seeing Jesus after the Resurrection, wedding celebration joy, the "birth" of a butterfly, a flower garden or tree becoming more, being touched and healed by Jesus.

Drama

The adding of words, often ad lib, to a simply-gestured gospel story or narration related to the lesson, the adding of simple props and costumes to aid expression. Possibilities for creative drama include the Christmas story, the calling of the apostles, The last Supper, Thomas' encounter with Jesus Drama includes miming Truth learned, such as the sowing of seed, Jesus in His carpenter shop or asking someone for forgiveness – all appealing to primary children. The Stations of the Cross for older children who might take various roles and present the creative drama as a prayer with a larger group in a common gathering place.

Creative Writing

Creative writing takes on many forms for young learners.

The individually styled, free expression of thought about a Truth learned or an idea held needs not necessarily be in a rigid, grammatical form, or correctly expressed at primary level. Thoughts might be expressed in three or four sentences on topics about receiving Eucharist, "my wonderful family" or "what I am learning about." Older children enjoy Pyramid poems: one word at the top; two words telling something about the word, on the second line; three words describing the one word, on the third line; a sentence filling out the meaning of the top word, on the fourth line. Handmade, individually designed booklets might collect learnings, prayers, or contain thoughts on a particular topic. Making one's own simple book appeals to young students who enjoy illustrating their writing.

II. The Visual Arts (those having 2-dimensional quality)

These are expressions which reveal in a concrete way that which is perceived as abstract. 'Artiness' is not of major concern since the child is simply expressing in tangible form that which he intuits in faith. Self-expression of understanding should be encouraged.

Painting

The use of watercolors or tempera paints to capture the unique response to a learning, a gospel story or a "chord of faith" being struck within the child. The teacher's tactful suggestion of composition qualities may help. A total respect, however, for the freedom of expression which is at work in the child is paramount to his faith-building through painting activities. Try the technique of blow-with-a-straw painting to express storm, various feelings or creation and God's power.

Torn Paper

The use of small scraps of colored paper to create a visual message for example, lettering on a large poster or banner, a frame around a special picture or piece of writing. Primary and older students are quite adept at tearing up scraps and fastening them to a surface with a dab of glue. One's NAME might be so expressed in lessons on Baptism. The words LORD, LOVE and GOD can boldly proclaim the concept being learned. A great way to recycle scraps, too!

Crayoning and Felt-penning Pictures

The creation of a picture using crayons of various sizes, including broken and peeled for their broad stroke effect, and various widths of felt tip markers. Both media have long been a favorite of children. The key to this media as effective in faith expression is the respect for the freedom to create one's own image, not to color someone else's rendition. There are no lines required of creative children to stay in.

Colored Chalk Pictures

The use of colored chalks to create murals on the blackboard or for individual pictures. The tones of color are usually soft and appealing. Outlining one's picture in pencil might help primary children begin confidently. Chalk rubs off its surface easily, so protections such as wet paper towel and smocks should be provided. Use a light spray of acrylic fixative to protect pictures after completion. For effective creations, use black or very dark-colored paper with pastel chalks and light colors of paper with dark shades of chalk. Use these attractive chalks, too, for blackboard messages for sheer variety.

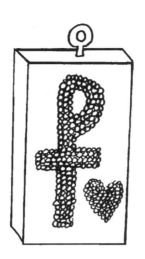

A mosaic of seeds and beans becomes a hanging to inspire and enjoy

Mosaics

The use of rice, beans, seeds, pebbles, crushed eggshell and coarse sand (which can be colored with a few drops of food coloring!) to portray Christian symbols, such as the cross or fish or to create only parts of a picture. Make small plaques for these out of heavy cardboard or wood, with a hole or hanger for a bright ribbon. Glue for the plaque is easily managed when it is watered down and applied with fat paint brushes. Spray creations with varnish to add 'hold.' Try a torn paper mosaic with primary children expressing "glory," heaven, God, power or other abstractions. Use a mosaic as a background for mounting a painting or crayoned picture.

Murals

The use of paints, chalk, crayon, magazine pictures or other materials on large sheets of butcher paper to express a story, a sequence of events, the current liturgical season, etc. Sufficient discussion beforehand will help students to visualize the creation. Murals can serve as a very unifying activity for middle and upper grade classes.

A Giant Filmstrip

The use of a long strip of heavy shelf paper, two paper towel dowels, and a "screen" made of a large cardboard carton to show a story in several sequential pictures, or to illustrate several parts of a whole subject (example: the seven sacraments, the corporal and spiritual works of mercy). Children's pictures might be glued to the strip, or the strip might be made in mural form. Cut a narrow hole the width of the paper strip on each of the two sides of the box. Cut out a viewing square on the front of the box. Decorate the box with lots of imagination. Thread the filmstrip through the 'theater' holes, and secure both ends of it onto the dowels for easy rolling through the viewing area. With a little practice, the children will delight in doing their 'show,' perhaps for parents or other groups as a summary of what they have learned. For "special effects," darken the room during the show and have a bright light shine only on the screen.

A Collage or a Montage

The use of various pictorial objects or other media to depict a theme; for example, Marriage, Family, Love, Church, Our Parish, Works of Mercy. A collage is a collection of things different in texture or material, a montage is a collection of things which are similar in material. Either expression can become an individual or class activity, perhaps culminating a particular topic of learning. Heavy cardboard works best for holding the glued objects firmly in place.

Bulletin Boards

The display of a particular theme, of children's work and learning activities or of attention being drawn to a special matter. For primary grades the theme should be kept simple, uncomplicated. A suggestion: center a large cardboard silhouette of a church, surround it with colorful houses bearing each child's family name, attach each house (connecting it visually) to the church with a length of colored yarn, completing the theme "We Belong to the _____ Parish" which is boldly lettered around the whole scene. Encourage the students to add flourishes such as pets, flowers and trees. Seasonal themes might show a Jesse Tree (Advent,) "Easter People We Know" (pictures and names of people who show New Life characteristics), "the Works of Mercy Show Our Love." Add pictures, symbols and other depictions to express the given theme. Children's creative writings should be set against colored paper or (a novel idea!) mounted on a sheet of wallpaper, accompanied with a boldlylettered theme title.

Banners

The use of fabric or heavy paper to portray an understanding of a learning. Banners might be made to carry out the theme of a liturgical season or to visualize a verse from Scripture. First sketched on paper, banners, should be kept simple and have large, bold symbols and lettering. Attractive color combinations are always appealing. A cooperative group project for young children, a banner might become a prayer focus at a liturgy or other gathering. Try mini-banners, each expressing a single word or Scripture verse. For these, older children might use parchment paper, tongue depressors and yarn for their inklettered projects. These banners might decorate a large branch, or be given as a gift.

Paper Crafts

The use of construction paper and other weights of art paper for creating learning activities in faith education. Many religion texts and activity handbooks for this purpose are ready sources for ideas in paper crafts. The following suggestions, too, will add like to children's learning through a 2 -dimensional visual creation.

A slice of "Jesus Bread." The child cuts out of tagboard a 7″ by 8″ slice of bread. Two parallel slits, each 2 ½″ long, are cut horizontally in its center, these spaced 1 inch apart. Above the slits, the child prints I BELIEVE JESUS. Below the slits is printed ME, THANK YOU. JESUS. Accompanying the slice is a strip of similar paper, 2″ by 9″ long. On the strip, the child prints words telling actions of Jesus toward the child: LOVES, LISTENS TO, HELPS, HEALS, FEEDS, COMFORTS, EMPOWERS, etc. The strip is threaded through the bread's slits, from back to front to back. As each action word becomes visible, the child reads the whole message, proclaiming: I BELIEVE JESUS (LOVES) ME. THANK YOU, JESUS. This activity becomes a wonderful prayer, too.

Mustard Seed Bookmarks. On each 2″ x 7″ bookmark is printed a Gift of the Spirit Word (from Gal. 5:22,) printing first very tiny, progressing to large, proclaiming the Mark 4:30 affect of the Kingdom "seed" within the child. Scotch tape a glorious mustard seed to the bookmark for impact and influence.

"Our Wonderful Hands Can." Two exaggeratedly-large hands are cut from stiff art paper. Glue each hand to a tongue depressor for holding, waving and showing their 'good news' to others. The child prints on both sides of each hand a great number of words which tell the actions which our wonderful hands can do: shake, lift, push, pray, write, etc. using several bright colors adds excitement to the result.

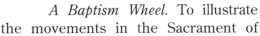

A Baptism Wheel. To illustrate the movements in the Sacrament of Baptism, the child is given a light-colored circle of paper, 10″ in diameter, a 1½″ x 4½″ strip for making an arrow, and a brass paper-fastener. The circle becomes a wheel, as it is lined with 8 evenly divided sections. The child numbers them from 1 to 8, and imprints into each section an appropriate symbol and brief explanation of the movement in the Sacrament, such as:

1.   (a church with people)
      I AM WELCOMED INTO THE CHURCH
2.   (a cross)
      THE CROSS IS TRACED ON ME BY MEMBERS OF
        THE CHURCH
3.   (holy water)
      HOLY WATER IS POURED ON ME, A SIGN OF LIFE
4.   (holy oil jar)
      I AM ANOINTED WITH HOLY OIL
5.   (white cloth)
      A WHITE CLOTH IS PUT ON ME
6.   (an eye, an ear and mouth)
      I AM "OPENED" FOR THE LORD
7.   (a lighted candle)
      I RECEIVE THE LIGHT OF CHRIST IN MY LIFE
8.   (triangle or three rings)
      THE GRACE OF THE TRINITY IS IN ME

With a small hole made in the center of the wheel, the arrow (pointed at one end) is attached to it with the paper-fastener. The progression of movements in the Sacrament become easily understood as the wheel is turned and its symbols and explanations are interpreted. (Such a wheel, greatly enlarged, can be a great visual aid for Baptism lessons.)

III. More Visual Arts (those having a 3-dimensional quality)
With such expressions, creativity abounds and is very satisfying. From fold-

ing paper, modeling clay, and arranging objects to puppeteering, baking and miniature church-modeling, the MAKING of things fascinates and, above all, impresses learning for children.

Build Things

Create an "upper room" for Holy Week and post-Easter learning. A large box, turned with one side open; folded paper for stand-up apostles, and Mary; small boxes and scraps of fabric for furniture; small clay eating vessels and "food" all create the scene for the coming of the Holy Spirit, the church's beginning. Have tiny flames ready for the heads of those waiting.

An Advent Wreath for the classroom, following some researching of its meaning; have all contribute to its creation.

A Classroom Paschal Candle. With tiny pins, attached several New Life symbols to a stout candle to be used at prayer time during the Easter Season. Similarly, a Holy Spirit candle, bearing the printed gifts and fruits of the Spirit, can grace a prayer corner during the Pentecost season.

A Model of Your Parish Church. Using a large, shallow carton create this powerful visual impression. Following a tour of the church and making a list of important interior furnishings, children might use small boxes (for the altar, lector's stand, tabernacle, benches, baptismal font, etc.) to image their church, setting items into their appropriate places. (See Chapter 7 for more details.)

A Grace Fence. Erect a low "fence" of cardboard on a tabletop with the sections locked together by slits at the end of each panel. Glue or paint on flowers to the inside. Write "We are baptized, we belong to Jesus, He will keep us from evil and harm," or other expressions of God's care on the outside of the sections. The fence illustrates the gift of Grace, and becomes an enclosure (with a gate for all new comers, of course) for the children's paper cut outs of themselves.

Make Things

Puppets. Keep them simple. Paper-plate faces, or use a round (salt) box with a dowel holder, yarn "hair," felt cutout eyes, head coverings of small pieces of cloth for Biblical characters. Try tongue depressor people with popsicle sticks for arms, dress this with paper or cloth 'slip on' clothes, Styrofoam balls for heads with poke pins holding felt cutout facial features; dress these with cloths wrapped around a dowel (which becomes the holder) poked into the head.

Try a paper sack puppet: draw facial features first, fill with crumpled newspaper, gather over a paper towel dowel, tie securely.

Sock puppets just feel like fun! Decorate with felt scraps after filling with batting. A hat made from the toe of a sock makes a character. Many good resource books are available for puppetmaking, which is an all-time favorite learning tool with young children.

"My Baptism Treasure Box" made out of any box having a lid. Cover with white paper, decorate it with Sacramental symbols. Keep "treasures" inside, such as a paper candle, a certificate with true data, a child's

baby picture, a paper or cloth baptismal robe or any other learnings gathered in their study of the Sacrament of Baptism.

A "Jesus Cares About Our Families" Box for the classroom can be made out of an Oatmeal box, covered with plain, light-colored paper. Each child glues on the box a panel depicting his/her family. Each panel of paper holds buttonheads for family members, stick figure bodies, and names of individuals. After completion, the children write their prayers and petitions for their families, using a colorful notepad and pencil kept handy inside the prayerbox. Give this helpful prayer-prompter a special place in the room.

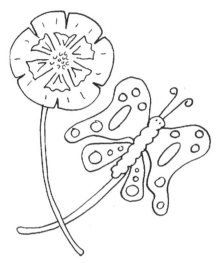

Attach huge butterflies, lavishly decorated to strong, supple wire. Hold a joyous fly-in celebration after Easter, to express the joy of new life of the Resurrection. Papersculpt large flowers, attach to strong wires and enjoy these megablooms in a spring creation celebration.

A card embroidery picture shows off those Christian symbols learned. Child traces outline of a fish, cross, bell, star, candle, drop of water, etc. onto medium-weight tagboard; marks dots ½ in. apart all around a penciled symbol; punches holes with a small nail and threads colorful yarn in and out of holes, taping the beginning and ending of yarn on the back of card. Attach a paper clip for hanging in a prominent place.

Plaster-of-Paris Plaques a satisfying activity for children of all abilities. Pour into a jar lid, or other discardable "mold" which has been lightly greased with salad oil, enough prepared Plaster-of-Paris to fill it even with the sides. Set in a paper clip for hanging. Poke into it while soft some little dry flowers, pods or shells whatever fits your theme. Etch into the plaster one's designs, initials or other impressions while it is soft. When thoroughly dry and hard, carefully remove the plaque from the mold, paint it, or bind it with ribbon if desired. These make lovely hangings for celebrations of Mary.

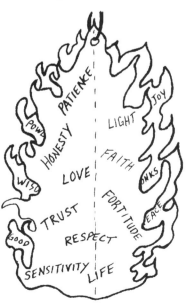

Celebrating the Holy Spirit calls for bright, colorful flames! Make them as ornaments to be hung on a branch, or dangled mobilestyle from a rod. The child cuts a flame freestyle from each of yellow, orange and red pieces of construction paper, about the size of one's open palm. The three flames are held together, and a vertical staple is put in the center, creating one single flame. The two outside flames are folded away from their center, creating a three-dimensional look. Punch a hole in the topmost point of flame to hold a length of yarn for hanging. The gifts and other blessings of the Holy Spirit might be imprinted on the flames: power, light, joy, love, strength, faith, courage, etc.

Giving thanks for the gift of sight is irresistible with childmade "binoculars." Cover two toilet tissue dowels with brightcolored paper. On another light-colored piece, 3″ by 11″, the words of thanks and appreciation for sight are written. Tape the two dowels together, and wrap the long piece around them, to create binoculars which are enjoyable to peer within one's new gratitude for sight.

Windcatchers, too, help celebrate the Holy Spirit! The child decorates very lavishly a piece of white paper 4½″ by 5½″ in size, then glues it securely around a toilet tissue tube. Holes are punched in a row around the bottom of the tube for the child to tie on various lengths of ribbons, yarns and even tiny bells to the ends of these. Punch two holes at the top for a length of yarn for hanging the windcatcher on a tree-branch where it will, indeed, 'catch' a passing Spirit-breeze.

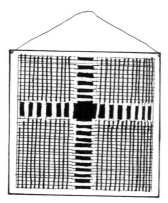

Weavings have long satisfied youngsters. How about trying *unweavings*? Simply give the child a rectangular piece of colored burlap, about 7″ x 9″. To unweave a cross, begin at top center and pull out several threads, one at a time, from the burlap for the vertical part of the cross. Next pull the same number of threads to form the horizontal part of it. After a cross is literally unwoven, insert a length of colored ribbon weaving it into the spaces vacated by the pulled threads. Trim the ends even with the size of the burlap piece. Mount the activity onto a firm piece of white cardboard which is a bit larger than the piece of burlap. Give it a ribbon at the top for hanging.

A Relief Map of Palestine can be made in a shallow, sturdy box about 15″ x 20″ in size. Using the salt-flour clay medium (see page 49), spread it about 1½ inches thick in the box. Following an authentic map of the region, impress its lakes, hills, seas and rivers. Identify major towns and cities, and even the events in the Gospels which happened in them; write these on small signs and mount them on fat toothpicks. Insert them into their places while the clay is still soft. When completely dry the map may be painted to further identify terrain. A great activity for a class of 5th to 8th graders.

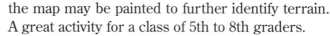

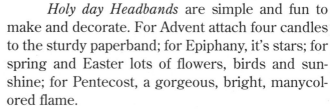

Holy day Headbands are simple and fun to make and decorate. For Advent attach four candles to the sturdy paperband; for Epiphany, it's stars; for spring and Easter lots of flowers, birds and sunshine; for Pentecost, a gorgeous, bright, manycolored flame.

Papier-mâché used as a medium for making symbolic shapes such as the Lamb of Victory at Easter, or any desired 3-dimensional object such as a puppet head. Begin by covering an appropriately-sized box or balloon with small strips of newspaper dipped in a bowl of wheat-flour paste. Continue wrapping it to form the desired shape, drawing out the image desired by filling in spaces with small strips of the paper. Let it dry thoroughly, then paint the object as desired. Add 'hair' to the puppet head. Older students enjoy meeting the challenge of papier-mâché.

IMAGING AS ESSENTIAL IN FAITH TEACHING

In closing this chapter, with its considerable emphasis on the shaping of a great lesson, we will return to a principle which underscores all that has been said regarding the importance of the faith learning environment, the manner of the presentation of the Truth, the full engagement of the learners, and the creative expression of the interiorized Truth. *We reemphasize, therein, the critical issue of employing and enjoying images, or signs, throughout a great lesson.* We refer to those visual, auditory and tactile aids which help to introduce, engage, allude to and enter into the Truth and Mystery being revealed and received within the child. In simple terms, we might think of images as those things which a child allows to lead one into the place within, where the Mystery and truth are being revealed.

The very language of images speaks beyond our limited verbalizing in their intent to open one's intellect and spirit to the message presented. Images are like 'keys to the heart,' where the Truth awaits to be affirmed. How vital is the catechist's employment of images in a "great" lesson? Since children readily interpret the language of symbols and images, we have seen their use as simply, no less than critical to the faith education of their young hearts! Open to the Truth which images reveal, children easily intuit and translate their inferences. Indeed, the child open to the Spirit has an innate hunger for the reference of the image, a hunger which is satisfied in the ultimate pondering and claiming of the message first encountered through one's sensory avenues. The receptive child is profoundly capable of going deeply within, to probe the Spirit's promptings and to intrinsically affirm and reverence the Truth revealed. Therein, one is most naturally and truly integrated as God's created child coming to faith from within. Images, then, are those means for the creative catechist to capitalize on in leading the child who, through the exercise of imagination and intuition, enters evermore deeply into the Truth and Mystery within. Our spoken words, although valuable and necessary, cannot, in themselves, make the young heart fully receptive. The heart is, undeniably, on a level deeper and richer than uttered language can reach. It is in our proffered signs and images where the child is able to discover and claim that Truth which awaits within one's inmost being. The catechist who honors this principle is satisfying the child's spiritual need in a manner far beyond the efficacy of any other method.

"The method of signs knows that human language is always an approximation," writes Sofia Cavalletti in *The Religious Potential of the Child* (Paulist Press, Ramsey N.J., pps. 165–166.) Further, she confirms, "At the same time, it is a method full of respect for the person and his capacities: in contradistinction to the definition, which must be received by everyone in the same way and at the same time the sign, which creates space for the individual's personal work of absorption, will be penetrated by each person in a different way – obviously within the limits given by the sign itself – and at a different rhythm.

Cavalletti continues, "The method of signs is very helpful for the catechist. When it is correctly used, it is impossible to overcontrol the child. In order to exercise control there must be a common measure, and this cannot exist when we use signs, when we try to help the child to enter into the mystery. The catechist who uses the method of signs will find himself in a position of extreme poverty in comparison with the person who holds the apparently secure tools of control; but his poverty is the richness of faith."

It is when the faith lesson is replete with images and signs – appealing pictures and figures, interesting articles for handling, textured surfaces, colorful hangings, contributory sounds, inspirational music – that those moments of development become, indeed, great, for it is through such necessary paths that the child walks freely, and that one's hunger and thirst for the ultimate knowing begins to be fed, truly nourished and satisfied.

"I just say
what I want to say to God,
quite simply,
and He never fails
to understand."

St. Theresa of Lisieux

6

HELPING CHILDREN TO EXPERIENCE PRAYER

The young children gather in a circle at the close of their lesson. In their center is a card table. Reverently they begin to 'set' the Prayer Table for a few moments of reflection. Two children lay the prayer cloth which several others have creatively decorated. One arranges a Children's Bible, open to the passage which another will read. One child affixes the large prayer candle in its stand. Yet another places a bouquet of flowers brought from home. Several children hold cards on which their prayer is printed in their own words. A child turns on the tape recorder's soft music. With the teacher joining the circle, modeling a quietly centered readiness, the group's prayer begins. The prayer's theme is impressed and expressed as the children listen and speak.

+ + + + +

A large white posterboard heart hangs suspended in the classroom. On it is printed the Lord's Prayer, each line a sequential color of the rainbow. The primary children gather before it, prayerfully reciting its message, gradually committing it to memory. Several weeks later the Hail Mary will be similarly printed on the heart's reverse side. Prayerful repetition will again commit the words to memory.

+ + + + + + + + +

A group of boys and girls who are preparing to receive First Eucharist have just learned about the Presentation of the Gifts at Mass. Their lesson concludes with their prayerful singing of A Gift From Your Children (Cary Landry, *Hi God* 3, N.A.L.R., Phoenix, Ariz.)

+ + + + + + + + +

Fourth and fifth graders gather to celebrate the Sacrament of Reconciliation. They sit quietly, prayerfully contemplating their hands as gifts meant for loving as their leader guides them in a meditation about hands.

+ + + + + + + + +

Primary children gather for a prayer in thanks for a newly baptized member of their class. Having seen the story of Jesus' love for children, enacted on a flannel-graph, they quietly ponder, and rejoice in, the love Jesus has for them.

+ + + + + + + + +

The young mother struggled to maneuver the car around icy patches of road as she traveled with her two young children on a bittercold winter day. Suddenly, the vehicle began to spin around in a seemingly uncontrollable manner. The mother stopped the car, and turned to her children and said, "Kids, we can't move with the ice on the road. We'd better pray." Her six-year-old daughter in the back seat then said, "God is great. God is good. And we thank Him for our food."

Thus do children experience prayer, experience the inner movement toward their God, experience the heart hearing the Divine voice.

Since, as their catechist, we are profoundly interested in, and committed to helping the inner movement of prayer to occur, it is well that we understand children's prayer and explore some possibilities for helping them to experience its activity. Surely, we hope that all will come to value and rely upon the power of prayer for their lives.

It will help us to promote prayer with children if we, as their catechist, first look within ourselves, and name what we believe when we say "prayer." Perhaps prayer has a learned definition which we memorized in years past. It might well have become a variation of a definition, one which has since risen out of our own life experiences. In whatever vocabulary we would name our idea of "prayer," we can rightly conclude that our own individual and personal concept of prayer is authentic. This is so because prayer, for each pray-er, is the expression between two hearts, ours and the Lord. In its truest sense, all our prayer, is worthy. All our prayer is 'acceptable,' for prayer is the voice of one's heart, which our God hears and understands.

Whenever our prayer is in a community context, such as in the family, a prayer group, or a liturgical celebration, it is essentially our personal inner heart-response which attests to our "prayer." If we are alone in prayer it is, likewise, our open-heartedness and inner freedom which activates genuine prayer. At the very heart of our concept of prayer is our openness to the object of our reaching out. Through our openness, born out of a certain necessary emptiness, we enter into that inner communion which is the very activity of prayer. Our seeking becomes a finding, and in it we are 'found.'

What is essential about ourselves as adults who experience prayer as responsive communion, is ever so applicable to children. The principle of heart-release and inner freedom is adaptable to them as pray-ers, a point which we witness in their sincerity and integrity during inner communion.

Let us recall that our loving God has created each of us for relationship, for response to love, for communion. In a broad sense, we as a people are being shaped as Church, as many becoming one; yet our loving creator has formed within each of us a singular heart for receiving God's love, and returning love in unique response. It is for each and every child to be convinced that prayer matters! Every individual voice needs, then, to sound its prayer. Indeed, our prayer completes our loving since it expresses so personally our response to love. In our own experiencing more and more fully the inner freedom and open-heartedness of prayer, we will convincingly promote for children this power for their own prayer, for what we will offer to them will flow from our own perception – and adventure – of prayer.

THE INFLUENCE OF THE CATECHIST'S ACTIVE PRAYER LIFE

As we continue, here, to develop some background understanding of prayer in our lives in order to bring to our children a richer and more rewarding experience of prayer, we will necessarily focus upon our own active prayer life and its ultimate influence in our ministry. Truly, our realization of the value and essence of our own prayer can effectively influence our children's devotion. The catechist's habit of faith-full, often creative, prayer will form one as a person of prayerful living. In our openness to the gentle breezes of the Holy Spirit ever calling forth our praises, thanks, petitions and repentance, we will all the more effectively teach that one's prayer is a natural outflow of the heart "in tune with God."

Essential in forming our prayer life is our conviction that all prayer gives praise to God. All forms of turning to God are praiseworthy. Well might we, as St. Paul says, "pray always." Practically speaking, our playing, working, studying, hugging, eating – all of living – can be lifted in praise by our momentary consciousness of giving praise. Truly, all of life is meant to be praise! For this we have been created! Into this flow of life we have been baptized. By the Bread of Life we are sustained for living in praise. Worthy is the catechist who leads children to see that right in their midst is "a burning bush' and that they are, indeed, 'standing on holy ground.' In other words, every place is a worthy prayer place. Blessed is the child who learns that his prayer can continually flow out in praise from the fountain of his heart. As their catechist, let us open children to this simple, yet profound reality that all of their life is matter for worship and prayer.

As a young child, I frequently walked open country roads and played in shady lanes with a handy swimming hole nearby. I can recall myself, during this idyllic time singing and speaking spontaneously to God. No one had taught me that such was a way to "pray." The sentiments just bubbled up out of a secure child's heart which thought that God (in whatever concept I believed at the time) wanted to know about what I felt. Indeed, these were probably the most genuine prayers I've ever prayed. The pure heart-to-heart quality I sensed still seems for me a strong sign of honest and authentic prayer. Its essence crystallizes for us the truth that we need not *teach* children to pray we need to learn from them how to pray, *how* to commune meaningfully with our loving God.

Our understanding of heartfelt prayer will be all the greater as we consider a second fundamental truth: Prayer changes us. Our dialoguing with God can reveal for us our particular internal health. Gradually, God's loving plan for us becomes clear. As we become more responsive to inspiration, our communion deepens us to live by faith, and to overcome that within us which is contrary to God's will. We become more the good in ground which the kingdom can grow. More open to correction, growth and to risking healthy conversion, we can begin to make the changes which Christ's inner life effects. Our beliefs deepen. Our convictions firm up. Our will for Christ's mission strengthens. Again and again, we are able to discover in ourselves, and in given situations, certain conditions which improve as a result of our prayer.

This is as it must be when we trust in the promises and teachings of the Lord. Prayer changed the men and women (who were as broken and as spiritually poor as we are) who submitted their needs, their sick loved ones, their repentant hearts to God. Surely, Christ would have us, too, realize that one of the fruits of faith is change, change in one's inner and outer outlook on life. How apt this is when we consider that prayer and praise place our hearts in Christ's own, *who is covenanted to us!* We are in Christ's will. We are in his mind, in *him!* His desire is to heal, to provide, to feed, to fill. His desire is to *change.* Because we are each His growing child, Christ's longing is to change us for reaching our fullness in Himself. Living in Christ, we will, be moved to welcome the changes effected by our prayer life. In truth, it is our faith in His word which we are called to both live and teach. Our excitement in helping children experience prayer is that together we believe *Christ lives!* That all He is is for *US! This* is the faith and catechesis which our children, perhaps quite unknowingly, hunger for in learning to pray. Let us, then, believe and "feed His lambs" well.

DEEPENING OUR PRAYERFULNESS

In addition to the suggestions for our daily prayerfulness given in Chapter two, let us consider further how we might deepen our own experience of prayer, of responsive communion with our God.

Set aside daily time with the Lord and His Word. Plan your everyday schedule to include your prayer time as the top priority. Be wherever you can best communicate, most fully receive and most heartily respond. Let there be much "sursum corda," the "lifting up of the heart." Offer your attentiveness to the voice of God speaking heart to heart.

Grow in an awareness of the Holy Spirit at work in your life. This calls for sensitivity, listening and observing the power of the Spirit in your mind, emotions and will, in everyday relationships and circumstances. Prayer 'tunes us in' to the subtle movements occurring.

Be prayerful throughout the day. Enjoy much ongoing inner dialogue and listening during all hours. Music, walking, reading and quietly "sitting" can allow God to bless us as the noises of life become still.

Often express your prayer creatively. Employ your inner resources of imagination, intuition, and sensitivity. Let natural objects (a shell, a candle, a plant, flowers, etc.) help speak your thoughts and lead you deeper within. Use gestures (bowing, lifting arms, kneeling, opening the hands, etc.) to express the heart. Move creatively to music. Write your thoughts in a prayer journal. Change your place of prayer. Sketch or paint what has moved within you. Sing! Laugh! Try various prayer styles (a litany, reading devotions, the rosary, the liturgical hours, repeating a single word, etc.).

Emphatically, begin right where you are comfortable in prayer. Perseverance and flexibility will promote healthy progress, and in them we can expect the blessings which will surely follow.

How, then can we as creative catechists, help the experience of prayer happen for children? The following guidelines can be applied in our classrooms and will easily adapt to various age levels.

THE PRAYER SETTING, AN APPEALING PLACE FOR CHILDREN

Everything about the atmosphere for prayer with children from the sound of the catechist's directives to the planned form which the time will have should help the young spirit to be relaxed, secure and open to the experience. The prayer-place should be familiar, comfortable, and without undue distractions. In a classroom, the prayer center described will serve these needs easily. If the group isn't gathered around one, they will do well seated in a circle. (I enjoy circles for their value of building community, allowing each participant to be seen and heard, and for the sense of equality which the circle imparts to children.)

Soft lighting and quiet instrumental music help to set the mood for becoming peaceful in body, mind, and spirit. If their own activities or other helps will be used in the prayer, youngsters will need to meet the challenge of managing the items while keeping their attention on the prayer and on remaining reverent. If the children are to remain seated in their chairs at desks, it is particularly important, in order to ensure their maximum attention, to arrange each one's seating position so that eye contact with the leader is possible. Desks and laps should be free of distractions. Postures of alertness and interest should be the expectation for everyone so that, even in the initial prayer setting, there is comfort and calm anticipation for the catechist and the children. When the prayer will involve some reading, and the children are using papers, ask them to be "in charge" as a responsible manager of the "quiet" they will insist from the papers.

WHEN PRAYER IS PART OF THE WHOLE LESSON PLAN

When prayer is included in the allotted lesson time, the catechist needs to plan for it to flow naturally and logically out of the lesson, reflecting the subject or theme of the learning. Typically, the lesson will include the presentation of a Truth. Then, and especially for primary children, to allow the Truth to dwell in one's heart and mind, a creative activity related to the Truth itself is included. Thus, the child expresses what is learned, making it part of their faith experience. In planning the prayer as part of the lesson, the creative activity can be incorporated into it deliberately, giving even greater value to the creative expression for the child. This natural integration will make sense to the child, who is allowing the Truth to become a part of his faith while crystallizing it in both learning and in prayer while it is 'fresh' and logically related to the lesson's context.

By way of illustration, a group of youngsters who were preparing for Baptism, had discussed the life of Christ within them as being akin to a small seed, a tiny thing holding unlimited potential. They concluded the discussion by prayerfully contemplating a small apple seed held in the hand, spontaneously speaking out about what they believed God might desire as their particular growth in Christ which would begin to 'sprout' with their coming Baptism. Their prayer was deepened by both the image of the seed as oneself, and by the spoken expectation of their inner 'seed' perceived 'coming to life.' (Such a lesson could also have included, for example, the planting of grass seed in a heart-shaped candy box. In the prayer flowing naturally from the learning, each child might then pray in petition for a particular desire for inner growth.)

Sufficient time must be a critical consideration when prayer is planned into the whole lesson time. Once the children's attention is focused on the prayer time, and expectations for it are clear, the sacred moments need quality time for the response and communion to be experienced. Hurrying any aspect of the prayer time will but subtract from the children's involvement and the expression needed for the full experience. Simplicity and brevity with depth of meaning are key guidelines for prayer planned as part of the children's lesson.

DON'T WEAR OUT THE CHILDREN OR THE PRAYER

Particularly if praying together is a relatively new experience for young children, it is wise to keep the time and their involvement brief. At first, perhaps only a few children will choose to speak out if the prayer calls for a spontaneous response. Those who do initiate some oral prayer tend to give other children confidence and encouragement to express themselves likewise. If students are asked to read a part, they should be given vocabulary which is familiar, and meaningful. Once the heart of the group prayer is achieved, it should move to a natural and logical conclusion. Brevity and clarity should be the guiding rule in prayer with young children. Older children in the middle grades or in junior high can be led in more extended prayer, and can participate more fully in both the prayer's composition and its experience. With the confidence which comes from repetition and familiar expectations, all children can, with our sensitive guidance, be drawn into deeper and increasingly engaging prayer times. The catechist, aware of the range of abilities, will offer them a variety of prayer styles, yet remain attentive to their need for genuine and meaningful participation.

INVITE IN A HELPER FOR PRAYER WITH A LARGE GROUP

Effective prayer time with children requires their attentiveness, concentration and sustained interest. Careful planning and clear expectations add to its success. Yet, even with these needs met, when leading a group larger than, say, twenty youngsters, it is advisable to have another adult present. Children falling slightly short of being 'angels' will reign in their tendencies to inattention when they sense the support of an added adult while they pray. Pre-arranging for the helper will be rewarding for both the children and the catechist.

When planning has been carefully done, and the time for prayer is at hand, one word expresses some sound guidance for what should follow: "RELAX." Simply stated:

"**R**"   Regard the children as people of God learning to pray.
"**E**"   Express prayer creatively at times, letting the 'tangible' speak with or for a person, bringing prayer up out of the heart. "**E**" also means

Enjoy child prayer! Emphatically!

"L"   Loosen up from any tension, and help children do the same.

"A"   Allow the Holy Spirit to lead your effort, and to join into the prayer time, calling upon God's presence in it.

"X"   'Xpect to "start small" at first. An underwhelming prayer experience can readily prompt the desire for more later on.

HELPING CHILDREN TO PRAY: WHAT MIGHT IT ASK OF US?

The Exercise of our Creativity

Out of our own freedom of spirit and creativity, we assist the children to free up the heart, and to respond creatively in their prayer. With our guidance in involving the powers of their senses, their imagination and inner freedom, children will be led to focus on and respond to an awareness of God within the heart. With the use of aids such as art materials, pictures, music, stories and even foods, we can bring children to know, value and, above all, enjoy prayer in their lives. What great delight this is for children once it is experienced. Pure faith is tapped. Joy in God is known.

Empowering children's prayer experience through the catechist's creativity implies our own inner vision as co-creators with God (for example, while gardening, baking a pie, carrying for the ill, stirring the soup or making a gift). As has been presented in Chapter One's thoughts about enjoying our gift of creativity, we realize that when our life-giving activities are perceived as our part of the unfolding of Creation, we ourselves are empowered to enjoy them, and can, as a catechist, all the more naturally assist children creatively with self-expression, particularly in prayer.

The suggestions for sensory stimulation to support children's prayer which are given here can become springboards for their involvement, and lead them to God's Truth and presence within them. Let us offer them such prayer prompters, born out of our creativity, as helps toward this end.

A bright red heart-shaped balloon taped to the floor in the center of the prayer circle, to symbolize God in their midst, full of life, beauty and joy.

Mobiles: of the Ten Commandments on stone colored posterboard, of large 'slices' of bread, each bearing a scriptural reference to one of the Beatitudes, each a colorful paper 'balloon' cutout, bearing printing on one side and the appealing smiley-face on the other, of cutout hearts varied in size and color, each side bearing a scriptural reference to love and forgiveness.

An Advent "coming" chain, each link having a scriptural reference with the word "come" or "coming" on it as each link is removed, it is discussed and incorporated into prayer. (See examples of these citations listed at the end of this chapter.)

An empty stable to hold tiny sheep, cattle and hay added gradually and prayerfully during Advent with the figures of the Holy family, shepherds, and angel added on Christmas Day, with the three Magi

A large heart-shaped balloon to encircle at prayer time

in place on Epiphany, coming to worship the Lord (who is then dressed in a tiny, royal robe, crown and scepter!) Expect much participation as the story is made visible throughout the Advent – Nativity – Epiphany season.

A Lenten still-life prayer prompter on a table, with an explanation near each item: an attractive jar of oil (the anointing at Bethany); thirty pieces of silver ('play' money suggests Judas' betrayal well); a large piece of "Easter" bread, perhaps familiar as "Pocket Bread," with a piece broken apart from it, a goblet of wine (the Last Supper); a rough, dirty piece of wood (the cross) a 'crown' shaped of thorny branches, a sizable rock (symbolizing the burial of the Lord) a lovely flower or a large "rainbow striped" candle (to symbolize the resurrection and the New Covenant of the Risen Lord). Added progressively, the articles will vivify the events of Holy Week when accompanied with appropriate Scripture readings.

A new life triptych made of three 'stages' of popcorn glued to a large sheet of cardboard, folded vertically into three equal panels. The first panel holds many unpopped seeds, images of ourselves given our natural life at birth. The second holds many popped seeds, symbols of ourselves baptized and "opening up" to New Life in Christ. The third panel holds many rainbow-colored popped corn, signs of ourselves in glory with God forever. Prayers of thanks and wonder flow readily when our 'story' is told in popcorn language.

A very large "hands of Jesus" cut from flesh-colored poster board and mounted on colored butcher paper for hanging banners at prayer time. Use in prayer as children attach their own cutout paper hand, a symbol of giving to Jesus praise, thanks, petition or repentance. The visual aid will adapt to any prayer theme, with children's writing on their hands giving even greater meaning to the concept.

The many sounds of nature on an audiocassette for background during prayer when themes relate to God's gifts in Nature, the seasons or creation play the compelling sounds of rain, wind, birdsong and thunder while gospel stories containing these sounds are part of the prayer use the sounds as background during meditative moments within the prayer.

A large, unsliced loaf of bread to be "broken" and shared by all, to embody themes of Unity, Eucharist, God's Goodness, and the like. Encourage tasting "to the fullest" with eyes closed during the eating, for often children retain the experience long afterward, when other senses are 'turned off.' Closing one's eyes during prayer can serve as a valuable means for centering inward, as stimuli are blotted out and one's focus is otherwise heightened.

How deeply we can bless our children in their prayer when our creativity comes into play. Our simple creations can help them to focus, to sustain interest and to actively participate in the moments. Most importantly, exercising our creativity in praying with children offers them necessary support which frees them to enter meaningfully and deeply into the experience.

USING OUR PERSONAL AND COMMUNAL RESOURCES

Resources of all kinds expand and enlarge meaning for learners of all ages. In our catechetical work, we are convinced that using visual and auditory resources helps youngsters to focus, and to enjoy learning and praying. Gathering or creating them (see Chapter Seven) is both exciting and rewarding. The catechist who builds up a stock of useful resources, such as a seed collection, pictures of every subject imaginable or a bare branch spraypainted white and anchored in a bucket, will find interested children at prayer time.

CREATIVE RESOURCES FOR PRAYING

Handbooks outlining prayer celebrations for sacramental, liturgical prayer or small-group gatherings are readily available from current publishers' outlets. Every program's resource closet should have several of these on each of the learning levels of children. Prepared, tested celebrations found in these manuals simplify the planning and designing of many prayer themes, and offer ideas for our adapting.

Consider, also, as an ongoing resource, a specific area created in the classroom as a "prayer center," a place where children will find a low table holding an open Bible, a statue of Mary or a Saint, a vase of flowers or greens arranged on an attractive cloth. Might the children have a hand in decorating the cloth, selecting the flowers and contributing additional prayer-prompters? Changed seasonally, or in accord with the children's learnings, the classroom prayer center can be an island of quiet, peaceful communion, indeed, a continual prayer resource.

The following suggestions are more prayer time resources. Gather, beg, borrow, make and save these for satisfying support for your devotions.

A really big rock to gather around, feel, think on Jesus' words to Peter (as Matt. 16:13-20 is being heard). Use the rock to center in prayer about Jesus' teaching that our faith 'house' be built on Him (in Matt. 7:21-27) or while everyone is praising the Lord, listening to Psalm 144, which begins with "Blessed be the Lord, my Rock!" Lots of sound insights should awaken when sensing God's presence in the rock.

Gospel "props" to bring to life the stories of Jesus and his teachings. A fishnet, a cane or crutch, a basket of loaves and *(real!)* fish, flowers, a well – branched ivy plant, a boxful of soil, a lamp, some mustard seed and a parchment scroll are examples of gospel visual aids. Offer them, and countless others, to young hearts at prayer.

A prayer tree a large "branchy" branch, set in a bucket of plaster of Paris. Use it to hang thematic symbols shaped as ornaments, or other shapes which hold written praise, thanks, etc. The branches might hold candid pictures of the children, which are incorporated into prayer. Attach prayers to the "bare" branches Holy week, then add many colorful, childcreated flowers which show new Easter "life." Pentecost's Fruits of the Spirit might be hung, having been written on colorful natural (paper) fruits. Bring the weekly learnings to prayer to hang on the tree, too.

Flannel-graph backgrounds and figures to visually enhance prayer when it is made from a given story. Children appreciate the creation of biblical scenes from which their prayer can grow so much more meaningful. Backgrounds can be made of flannel, and secured to a firm cardboard. Packets of figures (as well as backgrounds) can be purchased at religious supply outlets.

A large, plastic, heart-shaped bucket to use as a symbol of God, who, in the children's prayer, receives their drawings, writings or other creations placed into it. A "God bucket" might hold – and spill out – prepared messages to be prayerfully considered by the children. Check local hardware or houseware departments for possible sources.

A cocoon becoming a butterfly to await in prayerful awe during the Lenten season; to further children's concept of "becoming more" through our new life of Baptism; to prayerfully wonder at God's mighty 'work' in Nature.

Sand, tree bark, pretty leaves, shells, water, all for prayers of wonder, and for incorporating into prayer suggested from biblical references to the items. Add a *bird nest* and some *sheep skin* to these natural prayer resources; elicit prayerful responses to them.

Pieces or squares of carpet for sitting or kneeling upon during prayer time.

Several puppet characters a man, a lady, a boy, a girl, Jesus and other Bible characters. Use in prayer to help young children visualize a gospel story.

A "who is Jesus?" box. On each of six colorful sides of a cube-shaped box, glue a picture of Jesus as illustrating his "I Am" identities mentioned in the Scriptures. Christian resource centers and Bible picture calendars are likely sources. Print the "I AM . . ." near the picture which depicts the words. Learning these 'titles' of Jesus through familiarity in prayer soon makes an engaging memory game for youngsters.

Large sheets of coored butcher paper for creating a banner to express a prayer theme. Post the completed banner prominently during the celebration. Words from Scripture used in the prayer, symbols and other artistic expression on the banner can help lift hearts in worship.

The Jesse tree: our history in symbols on which to hang, during the Advent season, the symbols depicting the prophetic figures and events which preceded Christ's Nativity. Identify the prophesies in Scripture searches, or seek out books at Christian supply shops which identify and picture them for you. Create the symbols from art supplies. Hang one each day during Advent, as its Scriptural reference is read and prayerfully pondered. When all the symbols are hung, one sees at a glance the promised unfolding of the coming of the Messiah.

An "O" antiphon branch for hanging up ornamental symbols telling the Church's ages-old liturgical longing for the Savior, prayers which name the poetic titles of the coming Christ. These prayers are part of the Church's daily liturgy from December 17 to 24. Examples are: "O" Wisdom, "O" Key of David, "O" Rising Dawn.

At work, also, in guiding children in prayer must be our own inner resources. Our "catechist's intuition," enabling us to capture the Spirit-led moments in lessons which can draw learners into praise and thanks, can serve us well. Our particular enthusiasm "fires" us to continually move forward, using our gifts for the children's benefit. Our well-defined perspective, which clarifies objectives in view of the whole faith teaching picture, can help us to retain a healthy sense of humor and prevent burn-out.   Using our inner resources in helping children to pray surely rounds us as a sensitive, competent and creative catechist.

VARIOUS STYLES OF PRAYER WITH CHILDREN

How true it is: Variety is the spice of life. This maxim is especially apt regarding our helping children to pray in various styles of expression, since variety is the 'spice' of our prayer life, too. For the sake of interest, learning and faith development, the catechist will adapt several ways of praying to the needs and circumstances of the students. And there are several methods to choose from. Again, let your creativity be employed and enjoyed in exploring the various styles. Those suggested here might be used when prayer is part of a given lesson, or on separate occasions of prayer with children.

THE PRAYER SERVICE OR PARA-LITURGY

Used in the classroom, or in a larger group setting, this form of prayer is usually shaped around a particular theme or season of the Church's liturgical year. The style easily adapts to special occasions, too. At the beginning of Advent, Lent, or at the opening or closing of the school year, this form of prayer celebration fills out the meaning of the season as children express its mood and sets a certain tone for its observance. When the planning includes choosing the theme itself, selecting appropriate Scripture readings, choosing the readers, the responses, the group recitation and musical selections, the Prayer Service becomes a satisfying event for children. Participants should be given a written copy of the service, songs should be practiced beforehand, and banners created to accent the prayer's theme should be prominently displayed.

A Penance Celebration typifies a Prayer Service. Other examples include the blessing of animals (children's pets) in honor of St. Francis. More intimate gatherings, such as with one's classroom group, easily lend themselves to this prayer style.

One poignant occasion for me arose out of a special event in the lives of a group of second-graders. They chose to celebrate a "good bye" to one of their classmates who had died. (Though it was prompted by intense sadness in their loss, they truly felt it was appropriate to celebrate his new life in Heaven as best they understood it happening.) After a tender song, a brief Scripture reading, and spontaneous sharing of special memories of Jan's life with them, the children solemnly planted a tree in his memory, each child patting down a handful of soil around it. I am in awe at the depth of spirit which their catechist led the children to experience on that sacred occasion. At another time I enjoyed helping children with a small group Paraliturgy when a primary class celebrated one of their member's making of her Profession of Faith. Their prayer included a story of Jesus welcoming the children (depicted with colorful flannel-graph figures,) spoken prayer, song and all joining the child in the recitation of the Apostles Creed.

The prepared prayers at the close of most chapters of religion texts are further examples of the Prayer Service. They usually express the lesson's theme, and are an ideal introduction to this prayer style.

Many seasonal liturgy booklets are available to families who would involve members in table prayer, evening or weekly devotions or gathering in small groups for worship. When children experience prayer both naturally and habitually in the family setting, its value remains intrinsic for them through their lives.

MEDITATION

Faith educators have long acknowledged that children can be led to discover within themselves the power and ability to enjoy meditation, to "go down deep into the heart to be with God." Indeed, children are sometimes more able to achieve this level of inner surrender than are adults who can find it difficult to 'let go' of their control over the prayer experience. The good news is that once one overcomes inner tension and resistance, there is increasingly more comfort with this style of prayer, with its resulting peace, harmony and sense of unity with the Beloved One.

When children are guided to sit comfortably, with the whole body in relaxed control, it is possible for them to experience healthy and deep communion in their focusing, and to retain its lasting value afterward.

This form of prayer asks no words spoken aloud. It puts aside the need for expressing one's thoughts in verbal language. Simply, quietly "being," and consciously holding the sense of being the beloved of their creator, is prayer most praiseworthy, prayer truly freeing and creative.

When children are led into the heart-center of themselves, they are invited to let go of other attentions and to imagine themselves being in "God's great heart." There, secure in a love each has mysteriously experienced before the world was made (Ephesians 1:1-6,) they feel 'at home,' cherished, chosen. There the child may show God one's own heart, release to God any hopes, ideas, feelings and fears and may know the depth of God's all-encompassing affection. How uplifting and healing for today's child to experience, however briefly, the peace, serenity and renewal of meditation. How contributory toward creating one's personal relationship with God is the communion experienced in such centering moments.

The youngster whose body and spirit rest in the Lord, in the stillness of being loved, might enjoy "whispering within" one's special names of the Lord. Simply thinking of a favorite title, such as "Father God," "Jesus My Lord," "Spirit of Love" brings enjoyment from a level of communion which is both personal and potent. Older children experiencing meditation have recalled being inspired to speak the names "gentle fire" and "all creator." Out of their interior freedom during quiet centering, children are able to draw from the heart's well of spiritual energy and stimulation which becomes a delight to them when it is tapped. It has been well said, "Never limit the Giver, nor the gift."

Another variation of the prayer style of Meditation is experiencing one's sense of Wonder. Led through simple steps to relaxation – breathing in and out slowly and deeply, with one's mind and body in quiet control – the child focuses on a particular object being held, such as finds from a Nature walk, a stalk of wheat, some raw wool, a few shells, or several seeds. What prayers will flow from the child to the Creator of the treasure in the hand? What inner conversation will spring forth as these thoughts draw the child into God? Might the catechist offer children the experience of such prayer when the natural seasons of the year change, when the weather delivers rain or snow, and when treasures from an outdoor walk abound? Holding a fiery-colored autumn leaf in such moments, a fourth Grader once shared the insight that within the bright green leaves are the gold colors seen in her hand, that in the leaf's dying the real beauty began to show. "It's like us, when we do something loving the kingdom of God shows," she said, "but we have to die a little bit so it can happen." A child 'at home' within the heart!

SINGING IN PRAYER

For young children, singing a favorite song they have learned is a highly appealing form of prayer. They enjoy hearing the familiar maxim: "To sing is to pray twice." This prayer style seems to be a natural outgrowth of learning the words of a devotional song, perhaps memorizing them, and lifting the heart along with the voice in praise. Singing can easily become a part of a Prayer Service, or can, in itself, be prayer. This style asks but the sincere expression of the words, and becomes a delightful and compelling sound when offered reverently and with open hearts.

PRAYING WITIH GESTURES

This very creative style of prayer is enjoyed by children of all ages. In corresponding gestures of the head, arms, legs, etc., the child delights in the words of the prayer as one 'speaks' them with bodily gestures. This style is most often prayed in unison, adding all the more to children's pleasure and inspiration in its visual accomplishment. Each one senses a personal contribution to the group in the synchronized spoken word and descriptive gesture. The "Our Father" and "Hail Mary," annotated with gestures such as those suggested here below, exemplify this prayer style. Gestures might also correspond to familiar Christmas carols, freely 'made up' by the children once imaginative translation of the words is encouraged. Prayers such as Psalms of praise easily lend themselves to gestures of praise: raising the arms high and bowing low with arms crossed over the heart. The delight to children experiencing praying with gestures is that their whole self enters into the prayer, inviting a fuller and more meaningful communion of hearts.

THE "OUR FATHER" PRAYER

OUR FATHER, WHO ART IN HEAVEN,
(raise both arms high over head, slowly)

HALLOWED BY THY NAME.
(cross arms over chest, bow head reverently)

THY KINGDOM COME!
(arms form wide sweeping circle, coming together in front,
as in gathering in the whole world)

THY WILL BE DONE,
(nod head "yes," arms and hands 'draw' two halves of big heart)

ON EARTH
(arms and hands 'draw' big hills and valleys)

AS IT IS IN HEAVEN.
(arms high overhead, hands and fingers moving as twinkling stars)

GIVE US THIS DAY OUR DAILY BREAD,
(hands cupped, in front of chest, then coming closer to mouth)

AND FORGIVE US OUR TRESPASSES
(make a 'fist' and lightly beat the breast three times)

AS WE FORGIVE THOSE WHO TRESPASS AGAINST US
(in 'peace' shake hands with person on right and on left)

AND LEAD US NOT INTO TEMPTATION
(cover eyes with hands, shake head "no" in response to all evil)

BUT DELIVER US FROM EVIL.
(all join hands in circle, raise up high forming a 'fence'
to keep out all enemies of God's Kingdom)

**FOR THINE IS THE KINGDOM, THE POWER, AND
THE GLORY FOREVER. AMEN.**
(each raises hands, from floor to high overhead, end with a high joyous jump.)

THE "HAIL, MARY" PRAYER

HAIL, MARY,
(arms high and straight, overhead, facial expression happy)

FULL OF GRACE,
(arms make two full circles slowly, overhead, ending high overhead)

THE LORD IS WITH THEE!
(arms straight, slowly lower from overhead, palms open to 'receive')

BLESSED

(arms raised high overhead, palms down as in blessing someone)

ART THOU AMONG WOMEN

(arms lowered to front, kept straight, sweeping out to sides)

AND BLESSED

(arms raised high overhead, fingertips touching)

IS THE FRUIT OF THEY WOMB, JESUS.

(arms "cradle the Christ child," facial expression tender and loving)

HOLY MARY, MOTHER OF GOD,

(deep bow from waist, arms crossed over the heart)

PRAY FOR US, SINNERS,

(genuflect on right knee, hands in prayer)

NOW,

(elbows bent, hands one foot apart in front of breast, palms facing each other)

AND AT THE HOUR OF OUR DEATH, AMEN.

(palms together, hands at right cheek, head "sleeping" on them.)

THE DELIGHT OF MOVEMENT

A little resourcefulness in children's book shops will reward the creative cat-echist with suggestions for using *finger play* stories and poetry with young folks. These pantomimes can delightfully and easily convey the messages felt in the child's heart, and can satisfy the urge for movement, often involving one's whole body.

Be on the alert for other ways to help children express their hearts in prayer. Children love motion, they love to be in motion and respond eagerly to prayer which includes large and small motor skills. We respond to these needs when offering them a variety of prayer opportunities. Anticipate, too, that children are adept at creating their own gestures in interpreting prayer, a flair – and, indeed, a power – which should be encouraged.

SPONTANEOUS PRAYER

Prayer arising freely and voluntarily out of one's heart is, rightly, termed Spontaneous Prayer. As a prayer style, it can be a part of a more structured form, such as the Prayer Service, or it can be free of a predictable structure and used by itself. In either variation, the child benefits much from speaking or singing that which comes from the well of the heart. This prayer style seems more plausible when the children have been together for several sessions and are comfortable with one another. The sensitive catechist will gently encourage their participation by giving clear directives, and taking utmost care to avoid any intimidation to "speak out." The shy child might feel reluctant to do so; attentive listening and agreement is prayer, also. Happily, after a few experiences of Spontaneous Prayer, most children in a group are willing to share in it.

The value of spontaneity is in the freedom to voice what one feels and thinks about a subject while the concept is fresh and new in the mind. The idea springs from the present tense, and, by this virtue, it is truly created in the finest sense. The child at prayer is momentarily contributing something of himself which is both unique and precious. This is unquestioningly valued and appreciated by the creative catechist.

Spontaneous prayer might be made whenever children gather to give praise, thanks, repentance or petition. Usually, the catechist will lead into their offerings by introducing the purpose or theme of the whole prayer time. It is helpful if the catechist initiates, by example, the type of prayer expected from the children. Following this lead, they voice their prayer more easily. It is helpful, too, to young children, to plan an agreed-upon response, such as "Lord, hear our prayer," "Lord, we praise you," etc., be spoken by all after the individual prayer. This helps the next child sense when to begin speaking. How marvelous it is when children, in spontaneous prayer, confidently lift their words and hearts in faith to the divine Hearer.

MEMORIZED PRAYER

The religious educator concerned with developing children's full faith will pay serious attention to their need to memorize certain prayers. Long recognized as treasures of our Catholic/Christian heritage, some of the basic prayers committed to memory in childhood so become a part of one that they are retained (often instantly!) in later years. Rote has long served in our process of learning. It can do the same for our students.

Beginning in their early formation in faith, children should be helped to memorize simple prayers before meals, the Sign of the Cross, the "Our Father," the

Learning prayers becomes easy when a game introduces them.

"Hail Mary," the "Glory be," the Apostles' Creed, a meaningful Act of Contrition, how to pray the Rosary and Acts of Faith, Hope and Love. These veritable jewels in the heart's treasury of prayer become all the more lustrous when, once committed to memory, they shine forth in one's prayer life.

As children grow more and more familiar with the prayers of the Mass, being able to pray them 'by heart' gives the Eucharist celebration more meaning for them.

Let the creative catechist be inventive about presenting these prayers to children. Involving the senses in the memorizing is a great beginning.

Make an audio-cassette of reciting the prayers, play it to reinforce the sound of their own. Create large, colorful posters with pictures accompanying the words. Interest children in a prayer card collection. Find musical renditions of the prayers and let everyone sing along. Make a game out of the learning, such as spinning a dial on a board containing all the prayers. Create small personal booklets with individually designed prayer pages. Open and close their lessons with the prayers. Create a chart on which stickers are placed beside names of children as they memorize certain prayers. Memorized prayers can be a genuine source of deep and meaningful devotion.

Simple phrases, called ejaculations, should also become part of a child's inner treasury. "Jesus, Mary, Joseph, pray for us," "My Jesus, have mercy," "My Lord and My God," "St. ____, pray for us" and a number of the responsorial prayers of the Mass ("Praise to You, Lord Jesus Christ," "Thanks be to God" and "Glory to You, Lord," etc.) are, in their habitual repetition, easily committed to a child's memory. Blessed are they who are encouraged to pray these simple ejaculations throughout one's day, for in them lies communion and inner strength in need.

JOURNALING

A satisfying and creative avenue for prayer, particularly for middle and upper-graders, is the keeping of a prayer journal. To the student who journals, or "writes while on the path," setting down on paper what is felt in one's heart can be a valuable way of expressing and of releasing prayer. Encouraged to creatively design one's journal cover, and to 'talk to God' with one's pen, as well as note what one 'hears,' the student can come to know an often undiscovered depth of prayer communion. As a prayer style, journaling is personal and unique. Individuals may choose to write poetically, or in dialogue form. At times one may want to include a sketch beside the writing. Whatever relaxes the spirit and works for the young journalist qualifies as a success in this prayer style. The catechist should discourage any competition to outdo one another in journaling, and invite the students to share their prayer.

When might students journal in religious education? For those whose classtime is limited to one hour, and for whom journaling is the planned prayer form for a given lesson, it is suggested that five to seven minutes before dismissal be used for the writing. Taking a few moments to focus one's thoughts will help journaling to be more fruitful. Creativity will abound as young writers discover their own 'style,' use it as true prayer develop a variety of styles. Encourage the titling of a journal, perhaps borrowing a phrase from Scripture or other literary source.

One of the lasting values of journaling as a prayer style is in the student's own awareness of inner growth over a period of time, as the writings reveal one's increased understanding and perception of God as well as one's progress toward a deeper intimacy. This will be more apparent as the student continues to use journaling as a style of one's private prayer. Let personal journaling be promoted as a helpful, expressive style of prayer for youngsters.

SOMETIMES WE PRAY "JUST TO PRAY"

In the freedom of comfortable rapport flowing between students and cate-chist, there are occasions when unplanned prayer is a desirable and meaningful experience. In this mutual openness, prayer might be initiated by either the student(s) or the teacher, inviting the whole group to participate for a few moments. Perhaps some untimely news has disturbed a child. One might be trying to make a tough, important decision. Perhaps the catechist senses an undercurrent of conflict in the classroom. Even a joyful occurrence can be the cause of a prayer.

Any number of reasons might prompt a person to ask the group to join in brief supportive prayer. These spur-of-the-moment circumstances can be golden opportunities for prayer experiences which might offer release, and healing. The wise catechist will "take the pulse" of the situation which has arisen and offer the children an opportunity to pray (usually verbally, although written prayer might be an option offered) about the matter which has arisen. Let us not ourselves, nor allow our children to underestimate the *power* of prayer in any situation! Indeed, let their awareness of its power for them be one of our chief concerns as we help our children to experience prayer.

Our discussion of these varied styles of prayer leads us to encourage catechists to explore them with children. One might sense that a particular style would more 'suit' a certain group more than another form would, The catechist might be reluctant to try another style with them at all. Yet, it would be to the children's learning advantage that several types of prayer be introduced during the course of the year. Further, it is suggested that together the catechist and students evaluate their experiences of what has been tried, and be open to changes in order to have even more fruitful experiences in the future. To do so is to build up the value of using various forms, as well as to inspire the children to become involved in their own and their group's prayer development.

Many areas of creativity – drawing, writing, painting, drama – can be incorporated into prayer with children. Whether they are gathering as a large group to commemorate an event, ritualizing some learnings at the conclusion of a lesson or solemnizing a few sacred moments, it is the creativity which is brought to the prayer which can help it to have lasting impression and impact. In truth, the more involved the children are in 'making prayer,' the more deeply will they experience it. Creativity personalizes the prayer. It puts the "me" into the sacred moments, an essential ingredient for spiritual formation. The child who creates for prayer is saying in the heart "yes" to the invitation to "Come to Me." They are expressing that they *perceive* the Giver – God, *receive* the invitation to respond, *believe* in the Love being communicated, and therein, they *conceive* their response in prayer. It is in this responding to Love in prayer, in whatever form it will be released, that concerns the creative catechist, as we provide opportunity for its expression. Creativity, too, can be the 'spice' of one's prayer life.

TRY THESE 'PROMPTERS' IN PRAYER WITH CHILDREN

The following prayer-prompters incorporate both the catechists' and the children's creativity for the purpose of leading them into expressing what the heart is 'saying.' The suggestions might be planned into a lesson or used when a prayer activity can best express a given concept. Some prompters will easily lead primary children. Other ideas will satisfy the middle-grader's need. Several of them can be used during a liturgical season's observance. Their aim is to engage children in actively and constructively praying as well as personally experiencing some inner commitment to its purpose. Feel free to add to or alter the suggestions, using them as springboards to effective prayer with children.

PRAYING WITH COLORS. The children each choose a favorite color crayon. On white art paper, each illustrates one or several objects suggestive of the favorite color. Gather in a circle to hear each share the illustration created, telling why one considers it a 'favorite.' The colored objects may then be cut out and recreated into a collage on large butcher paper, or assembled into a bright rainbow of color for a bulletin board. Follow the children's sharing with their singing a "thank You, God" song for all the wonderful colors in our world, or with speaking a litany of thanks by praising God for creating one's favorite color. Enjoy primary children's enthusiasm and sincerity in this prompter!

FORM A LIVING ROSARY. Gather the children – several classes are usually needed to form this prayer together – around a flower-bedecked statue of Mary. Form them into the shape of a Rosary, with each child designating a "bead," and standing in the correct position. Each child, in turn, says the prayer which his bead represents, with all the other children responding to complete each prayer. Encourage their "big voices" so that each pray-er is heard clearly. This activity definitely calls for refreshments celebration at its close.

A "TERRABONNE" PRAYER CELEBRATION. The "Good Earth" loves to be celebrated! And held, smelled, appreciated and recognized as one of God's gifts to us! Have each child bring a baggie of soil from their own yard. Open them unemptied to share for observation, setting them together on a central table. Share observations of color, richness, quality, etc. Then have each child pour his soil into one large pan or waterproof box. Mix it all together, imagining God "creating the earth." Discuss various ways that the whole earth is a gift to us, especially how God's love comes to us through our soil. Water the soil slightly, and have the children have a part in planting some fast-growing seeds. Love the soil with water, and pray about God's power coming into the hidden dark of the soil. Marvel about the miracle of life which will produce root and shoot in the seed. Pray for bountiful harvest of flowers and radishes therein. Elicit awe in the soil's submission, and in the seed's cooperation with God's plan for it. Use Scripture such as Psalm 33's "The earth is full of the Goodness of the Lord," or Jesus' explanation of the Parable of the Sower in Mark 4. (Much of the Gospel of Mark lends itself to discussion of 'the seeds of faith within us' as related to forgiveness, God's will and Word, inner power, compassion, courage, generosity, etc. Look for ways to apply this Word to the meditation on seed, soil, growth and harvest.) Use pictures, too, to help children give their expression to feelings about the earth. Invite a "real" farmer in, to inspire their prayerful awareness of God's love of the Terra Bonne.

AN AQUABONNE PRAYER CELEBRATION. Rejoice in "good water"! (As preparation for this prayertime, have the children ceremoniously and slowly wash and dry their hands.) With the audiotape sounds of ocean waves or a splashing creek for a background, gather the children in a mode of wonder and thankfulness for God's gift of water. A display of pictures showing many uses of water, as well as its beauty, can help to draw their attention. Within handy reach, have a clear glass bowl of water and paper towels, as well as a pitcher of ice water with small paper cups. After some quiet listening to the sounds of water, and "looking with our spirit eyes" at the bowlful, begin with acknowledging the greatness and power of water on a natural level. Invite the children to quietly name some ways they enjoy and use water, and to thank God for its goodness. Mention the need which all of life has for water, and tell of God's provision in this need.

Draw forth deeper insight, then, into the water symbol of Baptism. Allow the children to share their knowledge or experiences of Baptism water being blessed and poured. Show pictures of a person being Baptized. Value together God's gift of baptism and its beginning of one's life in Christ. Appreciate Jesus' references to the water/life symbol by reading from John 4:1-29 (The woman at the well). Or listen to Jesus' teaching of water as a symbol of one being truly spiritually alive through service in John 13:1-20 (The washing of the disciples' feet). Older children can be offered Jesus' imagery of living in the Spirit as akin to coming to Him in our spiritual 'thirst' and expecting streams of living water to flow within us, heard in John 7:37-39. Allow time for all to "soak" in the Word about the spiritual gifts implicit in water.

Calling each child by name, invite them to dip their cupped hands into the bowl of water, once to see and marvel, again with eyes closed to truly feel its wonder. Help them to know its goodness with the power of the senses. Help them to be reverent, slow and quiet during these prayerful moments.

After drying hands on a paper towel, each child may drink some of the ice cold water, poured into the small cups. Again, lead them to "knowing its goodness" through the senses, perhaps with eyes closed for a portion of this time. Once all are seated, reflect together on any insights or feelings noticed during these experiences with water. Reflect together on God's Word about water's gift, and what might have been poured into one's heart during the listening and reflecting. Conclude this celebration of "Good Water" with all giving either silent or verbal praise to God for the gift of water for both our natural lives, and as a sign of our spirit-lives in Christ.

A LUXBONNE ("Good Light") CELEBRATION . . .
Follow the pattern of the Aquabonne celebration, using *light* as the focus. Let a flash-light, a lamp or a patch of bright sunlight draw attention to the gift of natural and artificial light from God. Briefly experience the absence of light. Share experiences of having the need for some light when one was in darkness. Appreciate having seen "the dawn's early light." Move into deeper insight with references to God lovingly creating light (Genesis 1:1-15). Recall Jesus referring to himself as the Light of the world (John 8:12). Ponder who Jesus *is* that he has the authority to say this. Acknowledge the indwelling light of God's Spirit, symbolized by a lighted Baptism candle – a Light for our life journey – with each child recalling ways in which he/she has responded to the light within. Refer to several of the Scripture passages which proclaim the gift of Holy Light for our lives.

Exodus 10:21-23	Matt. 5:14-16	John 12:35-36
Psalm 36:7-10	Matt. 17:1-8	Eph. 5:8-20
Psalm 18:28- 29	John 1:1-14	1 Thess. 5:5
Isaiah 9:27	John 9:1-7	1 John 1:5-8

An activity which helps children to retain this prayer's impression can naturally follow. Expressing one's desire to "be a shining light" in the world, each glues a bright (florescent yellow?) star bearing his/her printed name to a black butcherpaper "sky." The depiction could also include scriptural refenences to light. Older students might print the references on big yellow stars, to be set into theirdark sky, glowing with a lettered proclamation of LUXBONNE.

A *"WONDER AND AWE" TIME.* With soft, instrumental music in the background, the children come to a table laden with gifts from Mother Nature – pinecones, shells, rocks, tree bark, flowers, birdnests, moss, leaves, etc. Each child selects one gift to 'sit with' in the quiet, to look at with love, as God does, and to simply wonder at the object's uniqueness. This prayer becomes an activity of the senses and of the heart, as everyone shares insights and 'wonder thoughts' about the items. Have all the participants lift high their gift in whispered, or spoken aloud, or sung, praise to its Creator. All look around and appreciate one another's treasure being held up. With a renewed sense of awe at God's creation and power, the children reverently return them to the classroom "Wonder Table."

"WHAT'S THE SECRET HIDING IN A PUMPKIN?" Ceremoniously cut a lid out of the top of a pumpkin. Record the children's guesses at the total number of seeds hiding inside it. Involving all the children, count the seeds, declaring as winner the one coming closest to the correct number. Award a small prize for ceremony's sake. While each child (having washed hands, now) holds a pumpkin seed, guide their thoughts and discussion to the hidden treasure within each seed – *life!* And from within that life, *more* life., *More pumpkins!* Who has given us such treasures? Why? What is God's plan for the small seed in the hand? Listen to Mark 5:30-34 (the mustard seed) teaching about the wonder and miracle of God blessing our

"seeds of faith." How will the pumpkin seed cooperate in making "more"? How might we cooperate with God's grace in allowing our small faith-seed grow for God's kingdom? Offer a time for quiet reflection to allow the children to 'own' their response to the questions and insights. Recycle the seeds by dividing them evenly among the children. Propose a variety of activities for their continuing prayerfulness.

1. Reverently plant some of the seed, tend them with love.
2. Roast some seed to munch during a special "seed story" time.
3. Make a colorfully decorated castanet from two small paper plates laced tightly together and filled with many pumpkin seeds. Use them as rhythm instruments to accompany some praise music.

PRAYING WITH THE PSALMS. Introduce the timeless songs early in children's faith development, explaining their importance in the worship of our spiritual ancestors, and of the people of God today. Use a children's Bible for translation simplicity. Have pictures and other sensory stimulators ready to assist with understanding. These psalms lend themselves well to prayer for children:

Psalm 23. Read the Good Shepherd image slowly. Offer pictures of sheep, meadow, streams, etc., to enhance memorization.Discuss the shepherd – sheep relationship, likening it to Jesus and the church. Have the children attach their cotton-covered, paper sheep to a lovely butcher paper meadow showing Jesus in the center, protecting, feeding and loving the flock.

Psalm 100. Read once through s – l – o – w – l – y. Add some 'happy' instrumental music. Read with strong declaration while the children walk around the room in prayerful procession, toward an appealing picture of the Lord Jesus in a special praise place. A delightful processional for 'beginners.'

Psalm 111 praises God's wonderful works. Prepare for praying it by drawing pictures of God's works in the world. All of creation may be depicted in it. Print the psalm on a blackboard, using various colors of chalk. Tape the children's art creations around the words. All recite the prayer-song to become familiar with it. Invite the children to choose a verse of it, and make up their own melody for it. (Give suggestions of your own for this.) Close the prayer with appreciating that each person present – and the whole church – is a beautiful 'work' of God.

Psalm 136 is prayer litany of God's great saving work among His chosen people. This psalm of thanksgiving might be 'broken' into verses among the children or prayed as a whole. Middle-grade Bible students will recognize the events as spiritual history. Their response, "for His mercy endures forever" might be sung or recited after each verse.

Psalm 148. This beautiful, picturesque "Hymn of all Creation to the Almighty" will draw first-rate praise from children. Provide them with a copy of the entire psalm, inviting them to choose a verse to illustrate. After the verses are imprinted on the pictures, hang them in appropriate order. A quiet reading aloud of the whole psalm, with all meditating on the inscribed artistic impressions, will allow the prayer to linger, and will prompt the children to praise God when they see God's many "wondrous works."

"HE CALLS ME BY MY NAME." Help children to value more personally the call to be a Christian apostle, a present-day Kingdom-builder. After listening to the story of Jesus calling his first apostles (Luke 5:1-11) and seeing pictures, puppets, or flannel graph figures of the story, the children create a mask of their own face on a paper plate. The mask should show the child's features in all of one's distinctive uniqueness. With curly-ribbon curls, lengths of colored yarn for straight hair, and construction paper scraps cut out for eyes, nose and mouth, let the details graphically show each one's identity. Attach a tongue depressor to the back of the mask for holding up to one's face. Help the children to respond to the "calling" story by dramatizing prayerfully their own being called to be Jesus' helper. The person chosen to be Jesus calls the others, looks at each child, speaks his or her name, saying "Follow me." Holding one's mask in front of the face, the child apostle comes forward to sit near "Jesus." When all are gathered around, offer quiet reflection time, with the sharing of ideas for being a faith-full apostle in everyday life. Recall that each is 'called' from Baptism to live as an apostle in the world, and that Jesus is always with each one, giving all needed strength and grace for doing His Kingdom work.

PRAYING WITH A STORY. Sincere, profound prayer can spring out of a heart which has heard a story offering a moral truth. The secret for this to happen for young children is in the catechist's skill in relaying a story, be it in the reading or in the telling of it. Children love a story well-told. They enjoy "getting into it" with their fertile imaginations. They particularly relish stories with a built-in lesson or point which registers within the spirit, sometimes with deep impact. The creative catechist will capitalize on this valuable vehicle for building up children's faith and prayer experiences, and will explore sources of tales, fables and modern-day parables for this purpose. The following story is an example of such a prayer prompter suitable for middle-graders. (The author is unknown.)

> *Once there were two ladies who were very good friends. They lived on the same street. They did many of the things which all good friends do — they visited together, shopped, ate meals in each other's homes. And sometimes they argued together, which made them seem even closer to each other afterwards. The ladies' names were Mabel and Ruby.*
>
> *One day Mabel received a beautiful ring from her husband. It sparkled with jewels. The ring gave Mabel much delight and she wore it every day. Whenever she had a free moment she sat in a sunny window to catch the sunshine sparkling on the ring. Her heart seemed to grow lighter with her enjoyment of the lovely ring.*
>
> *On one sunny afternoon ruby dropped in to visit her friend, Mabel. "Oh," exclaimed Ruby, noticing Mabel's finger. "What a beautiful ring you have! How it sparkles in the light! You are certainly very lucky! I'd love to have a ring like that."*

"Yes," said Mabel, "It is a beautiful ring." They admired it for quite a while together. Then, much to Ruby's surprise, Mabel slowly and carefully twisted the ring off her finger, and held it in her hand.

"You are my dear friend, Ruby," she said quietly. "Here is my ring. I want you to have it to enjoy." Shocked, and speechless at her good fortune, Ruby accepted the gift, and put its sparkling beauty on her finger. The two friends hugged each other, feeling closer than ever before.

Several days later, there was a knock on Mabel's door. "Hello, Ruby," she said, smiling, as she saw her friend standing there. "Come in, and we'll have some tea."

Ruby sat down at the table while Mabel filled the tea kettle with water. As she did so, she noticed that her friend seemed very quiet, and in deep thought.

"I hope there's nothing wrong, Ruby. You don't seem like yourself today," said Mabel. "Are you enjoying having the ring I gave you?"

"Oh yes," Ruby answered. "The ring is such a pleasure to me." Together the two friends admired the sparkling jewels on Ruby's finger. "But well, you see the ring has helped me realize how very generous you are, my friend." Taking the ring off her finger, Ruby held it out toward Mabel. She looked at her and said, "And I really like having it. But I want to have something even greater than the ring."

Putting the sparkling fit into Mabel's hand, Ruby said softly, "I want what you have, my good friend. I want to be able to give the ring away." And she slipped the lovely band back onto Mabel's finger.

After hearing this story, the children should enjoy telling their reaction to the 'twist' at its end. Prompt them by asking: "What in the story surprised you? Delighted you? Challenged you?" Include in the discussion some character description of each lady, the qualities of their friendship and the value of loving generosity which Ruby gained. What is truly greater than having a material 'thing'?

The children's prayer might include reflection on their own friendship qualities. Spoken prayer might be petitional, asking God for grace to develop a particular quality as a friend, or for the increase in a certain virtue which the child feels needy for Christian growth. Thanksgiving, also, for those who have shown true generosity in the child's life might be incorporated in the prayer.

The following short tale is another appealing story which can easily prompt children's prayer, and help them to probe the wonderful mystery of "what can happen when we use our power to believe?" It holds much imaginative charm, which might be better drawn upon by inviting the students to listen to it with the eyes closed, in order to 'picture' its message unfolding: (author unknown)

A mother eagle perched on the edge of her large nest. Next to her sat her little baby eaglet. Soft, downy feathers covered its small , round body. They were a sign that the bird would soom be growing up, and doing the important things that growing eagles do. The two of them enjoyed sitting close together, feeling the friendly wind, and looking far and wide over the land down below them. The space seemed to be waiting for their adventures.

Several weeks went by, and the baby eaglet grew strong. His eyes cought the movements of small field mice in the grass far below the nest. He was larger now, and had longer, darker feathers on his wings. His mother enjoyed seeing his muscular legs grow strong, and the span of his wings become wider.

"I believe he is ready, now," thought the mother eagle. "Let us see what will happen."

Standing tall on the edge of their nest, and with a kindly glint in her sharp eye, she looded at the eaglet next to her. "Jump," she sail.

Her son stood closer to her, and a tremble went through his young body. "I'm I'm af-fraid," he stammered.

"Jump," said, the mother eagle again.

I'm, I'm afraid."

The mother eagle stayed beside her son, calm and reassuring. For the third time, the wise and loving parent said, as she stretched out her wide, strong wings, "Jump!"

And the young eagle did. And he soared.

There is enormous value in children sharing with one another the occasions when they, too, risked believing in the power of faith in their young lives. Invite them to tell about a time when they, too, had stood "on the edge, a little afraid to jump," and what the results of trusting and believing had been for them. How impressive their sharing of such experiences are. How effectively children teach each other. Conclude such sharing with prayers of thankfulness and praise, and perhaps petition, for the gift of faith in Jesus' powerful presence.

A FEW "AMEN" THOUGHTS ABOUT PRAYER

Out of curiosity, and for instructional purposes, I sometimes ask children what they think is the meaning of the word "Amen" in their prayers. Since I hear them say it at the end of praying, as is the custom, I often wonder if they have the true understanding of this little and familiar ending.

Replies to my question range from "the end," "I'm done," and "that's all," to "it's just a word, it doesn't mean anything special." Once a youngster amused me, though, when he said he thought "Amen" means "I gotta go now, God." Talk about creativity! All of which led to listing their possible meanings on the blackboard, and scooting around for resources to define the word correctly, such as an informed adult, and a Bible dictionary.

How rewarding it is for children to learn that when they do pray the familiar "Amen," they are really saying a great deal! Now they are consciously saying – and hopefully praying – "yes" or "I agree" or "Let it be so." Now praying "Amen" becomes so much more than a kind of 'door-closing' on the prayer. Indeed, it becomes an opening for the heart to let in more and deeper faith in the prayer it has just uttered.

As a children's catechist, we should continually affirm two essential truths about helping them to experience prayer: (1) that children are capable of a deep and sustained relationship with God through their prayer encounters, and (2) that, with sensitive guidance, children are able to develop a prayer life that is relevant to their lives. Prayer opens one to the wholeness and communion which even young children relish as they "get to know God." Later that very wholeness takes on a lateral growth as children are helped to experience a variety of prayer styles. Let us, then, welcome the many opportunities in our catechetical work which might lead to children's prayer formation. Let the creative catechist ever seek to stimulate childrens' natural responsiveness to the God dwelling within who delights in revealing Himself to all His children.

SCRIPTURAL "LINKS" FOR AN ADVENT CHAIN

"ARE YOU THE ONE WHO IS TO COME, OR ARE WE TO WAIT FOR SOMEONE ELSE?" Matt. 11:2-10

LET US BE PATIENT UNTIL THE LORD'S COMING. James 5:1-11

COME, LET US WALK IN THE LIGHT OF THE LORD. Isaiah 2:1-5

"LET ALL WHO ARE THIRSTY COME. ALL MAY HAVE THE WATER OF LIFE FREE." Rev. 22:17

THY KINGDOM COME. Matt. 6:9-13

"I HAVE COME SO THAT THEY MIGHT HAVE LIFE." John 10:10

"I, THE LIGHT, HAVE COME INTO THE WORLD SO THAT WHOEVER BELIEVES IN ME NEED NOT STAY IN THE DARK." John 12:46

LIVE IN CHRIST, THEN, MY CHILDREN, SO THAT IF HE APPEARS WE NEED NOT TURN FROM SHAME AT HIS COMING. 1 John 2:18

"I WILL NOT LEAVE YOU ORPHANS. I WILL COME BACK TO YOU." John 14:18

BLESSINGS ON THE KING, WHO COMES IN THE NAME OF THE LORD!
Luke 19:38

COME TO ME, ALL YOU WHO ARE BURDENED, AND I WILL GIVE YOU REST.
Matt. 11:28

"IF ANYONE IS THIRSTY LET HIM COME TO ME. LET HIM COME AND
DRINK, WHO BELIEVES IN ME." John 7:37

AND ON THAT DAY THE NATIONS WILL COME BRINGING THEIR
TREASURES. Rev. 21:25

"I AM THE WAY, AND THE TRUTH, AND THE LIFE. NO ONE CAN COME TO
THE FATHER EXCEPT THROUGH ME." John 14:16

"UNLESS I GO, THE ADVOCATE (THE SPIRIT) WILL NOT COME TO YOU."
John 16:7-8

"BUT WHEN THE SPIRIT OF TRUTH COMES, HE WILL TELL YOU OF THE
THINGS TO COME." John 16:13

"I CAME FROM THE FATHER, AND HAVE COME INTO THE WORLD; AND
NOW I LEAVE THE WORLD TO GO TO THE FATHER." John 16:28

COME HERE, GATHER TOGETHER AT THE GREAT FEAST GOD IS GIVING.
Rev. 19:17

MAY YOU HAVE MORE AND MORE GRACE AND PEACE AS YOU COME TO
KNOW OUR LORD EVERMORE. 2 Peter 1:2

YOU HAVE COME TO GOD HIMSELF AND BEEN PLACED WITH THE SPIRITS
OF THE SAINTS WHO HAVE BEEN MADE PERFECT. Heb. 12:23

COME, SHEPHERD OF ISRAEL, LISTEN. COME TO US AND SAVE US!
Psalm 80:1-2

COME, AND RESCUE ME, GOD! YAHWEH COME QUICKLY AND HELP ME!
Psalm 70:1

AMEN! MARANATHA! COME, LORD JESUS! Rev. 22:20

The "metaphysical" child
will find
the full realization of himself
only in the world
of the transcendent,
a world in which he has shown
he moves
completely at his ease.

Sophia Cavaletti, author of
The Religious Potential of the Child

7

BUILDING UP AND USING OUR RESOURCES

A few steps inside the second-grader's classroom, a large, vertical banner proclaims: *God loves to make life.* Surrounding the bright and bold lettering are colorfull pictures from magazines, portraying wildlife, pets and family life. A tall tree, a leaping fish, newborn twin babies, tiny forest plants and a litter of puppies are depicted invitingly. Each picture helps to proclaim the banner's message. Each is related to he children's life experiences. Each delights the seven-year-old mind and spirit.

Below the hanging "good news," a low table holds "please touch" articles which communicate more life messages to the students: two acorns, one closed, dry and hard, one in a glass of water, sprouting its shoot (which, it was decided, dreams of becoming an oak tree someday). Upon the gaily flowered cloth stands a pot of wheat seedlings which might one day become nourishing bread. A pair of goldfish cavort in a bowl of water. A bird's nest, an egg, a vase of flowers, too, announce *life.* A box lid holds seventeen different common seeds, neatly labeled. The children, having seen and touched the banner's Truth, readily receive it into their minds and hearts. Their learning of the meaning of Baptism's gift of life is tremendously enriched with each moment spent absorbing the display in all its natural wonder.

RESOURCES: VEHICLES OF TRUTH

During a typical Sunday Mass, the young children are led into their worship place to celebrate Liturgy of the Word on their understanding. Their catechist carries a large realistic looking scroll. Today the Good News will proclaim Jesus in the temple giving the prophetic message from Isaiah of His Messiahship. The scroll, carefully laid beside the children's Bible, will be opened and examined during their celebration of the Word. Unrolling a scroll will be a new experience in faith for most of the children. A deeper appreciation of today's scripture, through the power of their imaginations, will long remain in these young hearts.

RESOURCES: INITIATORS OF PERCEPTION

A cheery-eyed senior citizen stands before a group of middle-graders whose study has introduced them to the Old Testament books. Unfamiliar places, customs and language had typified the difficulties they encountered in reading the ages old texts. Out of the gentleman's recounting of his recent journey into the Holy Land are growing new, budding interest and blossoming familiarity with the historic scenes. From his slides presentation of prominent locales, the students are beginning to own their spiritual ancestry.

RESOURCES: OPEN DOORS TO NEW FAITH ROOMS

For the creative catechist, there is a profound conviction of the value of using all manner of resources in religious education. Their incorporation into our lessons directly reflects our sense of purpose in catechising children: that of opening them to what will help their spirit affirm and welcome the good news of faith. Our selection of tools for their faith-tapping work is virtually unlimited. Here, the catechist's imagination and creativity have full play! In full cooperation with the children's learning needs, as well as with their natural and intellectual attributes, the creative catechist will be ever alert to possible resources adaptable to a given faith lesson. Simply, we are challenged to use whatever will work leading one to presenting in concrete forms those spiritual concepts which lead to the treasured mysteries of faith. Further, as we are interested in honoring children's natural love of color, motion and form, as well as their delightful innate curiosity, we will not hesitate to let resources draw forth attentiveness and response. Sensory stimulation is the child's trustworthy usher into understanding.

The question which is ever-present during our lesson preparation is, therefore, "with what visual, auditory or tactile means will I present the Truth in the lesson?" Again, "how will I stimulate interest, active participation and cultivate faith in the good news being offered?" Surely, the answers are as multifarious as they are critical. We need but to be alert to their possibilities, and willing to explore them.

Before we review the use of resources regarding children's faith development we should, necessarily, reaffirm for ourselves the significance of certain resources in our own development as a catechist. For it is when we have grown in conviction, commitment and compassion that we become capable – and ingenious in leading children on the path of faith-fullness. In discussing the necessary ongoing faith development of the catechist in chapter two, effective resources were emphasized which aid one in faith maturation. Here, we will briefly underscore some of those areas of renewal which can lead the faith-filled catechist to even greater levels of re-creativity. We will understand that in responding to such available resources, one is cooperating with the Holy Spirit, whose work is ever to recreate us in Christ to make us a "new creation" in Him (2 Cor. 5:17). These inspiring and regenerating times of renewal can become for us a fountain flowing freely into our faith education ministry with children. Resourcefulness, then, can be viewed as streaming into, as well as out of the creative catechist. One needs but to be open to the power of its magnification in faith education.

RESOURCES THAT MAGNIFY

The following spiritual resources can help to deepen our reservoirs of inner life, from which we can offer our children nourishment.

Spiritual Reading – classical and contemporary writings which assist in developing an active spirituality and fruitful prayerlife.

Liturgical and Para-liturgical Services leading one to Scripture-reading and prayer which further open the heart and mind to Christ.

Adult-education Opportunities – classes, lectures, workshops which lead one to information, formation, and transformation in faith.

A Bible Study Group – for the studying, learning, sharing and activating one's *living* of the Word.

A Program of Parish Renewal – offering strength in the bond of one's community faith-commitment.

Retreats and Days of Recollection – for refreshment by, and a reorientation in, the heart of Christ through prayer, reflection and insight.

Prayer Group – for helping in centering one's life in the power of the Holy Spirit, and for forming a more teachable spirit in oneself.

Daily Prayer and Periodical "Resting in the Lord" – for developing a Jesus-sense toward all of life and its possibilities for one's growth.

One's Own Religious Education Colleagues – for growth in gift appreciation, interdependency and prayer-support.

These suggestions are but a few of the means by which the creative catechist can further one's necessary identification with the One, whose Kingdom, life and power we have chosen to share with children. It has been well stated that we can be a gospel teacher only if, first, we live the gospel. That, surely, is the challenge in Jesus' question, "_____, do you love Me?" Let us be unmistakenly clear that the impulsion to bring children deeper into their faith in Christ must be generated by our identification and solidarity with Him whom we present. This fidelity must be the premium stamp on our heart. Spiritual resources intend to form us as ever more sincere, willing and life-giving participants in Christ's mission. Indeed, let us be eager for this formation to happen!

RESOURCES THAT AMPLIFY

Within the call to be a Christ-centered, life-giving catechist is that of the classroom-oriented, ideas-generating educator. One who employs natural or learned teaching facilities. One who is willing to develop classroom management skills. Being attuned to such as the following offerings can make the vast difference between one's intolerable procedure and commendable achievement.

Many of these resources will help to broaden the content of our particular unit of study being presented to children. Others will be supportive as materials or personnel, which can help make our lesson procedure or presentation techniques more successful. Our vision of faith-responsive children can become more a reality in our use of these enlarging educational resources.

The New Catechism of the Catholic Church, called by Pope John Paul II a "reference text," the volume is replete with the church's doctrinal Truth regarding faith and morals. In its introduction, the Pope asks all the faith-full to consider the *Catechism* as "a sure and authentic reference text for teaching Catholic doctrines." We, as catechists who wish to deepen our knowledge of the unfathomable riches of salvation, ought to find in studying the *Catechism* a truly supportive and inspiring resource for our faith development. This bright light of Truth in our age will serve well as our guide to understanding (1) The Profession of Faith, (2) The Sacramental Mysteries: (3) Our Life in Christ, and (4) Christian Prayer.

Reference Books, Text Guides and Professional Journals are written specifically for teachers of faith, giving understanding to the process of education on various levels, as well as to the procedures toward reaching learning goals. Often such guides stimulate our creativity as well as motivate us to try alternative presentation styles. In these we will find help for improving teaching techniques, time management and classroom skills. Hear it from the experts, when you need fresh ideas, insights and catechetical inspiration.

Child Development Forums are settings which teach of the stages of growth in children, and which assist in reflecting wisely upon our youngsters' physical, emotional, psychological and spiritual development. The settings might be as varied and informative as a parent night guest speaker at a school or an informal gathering of parents, older siblings or experienced educators. The wisdom gleaned from both developmental authorities and "old hands" in child-rearing is a valuable resource to the faith teacher interested in the whole child.

Religious Education Conferences and Workshops. Whether large or small in scope, the ideas and inspiration generated from joining with one's colleagues in catechetics are enormously beneficial. Hearing from specialists in various areas of faith education unfailingly boosts one's morale significantly, for it seems the call to be catechist is one which needs to be answered anew and affirmed periodically in community. Visiting and sharing insights with fellow catechists invariably energizes the heart and mind. Truly, we are so much *more* when we are together! Often, too, the book vendors at such events can add to our resource libraries and supply closets.

Fairs of All Kinds abound in creative ideas. Come ready to make note of the new and 'different' arts and crafts, along with the tried-and-true cleverness in creativity. School Art Fairs particularly explode with creations which are adaptable to the faith-learning classroom. Puppetry, song, theater and dance can often be found as resource samples at such events. Family festivals, sometimes religious in flavor, offer excellent home-faith education resources. Gather all available hand out materials for your files. Jot down ideas for future reference. (Until I had seen the artistic possibilities of 'torn scrap paper' crafts at a school Art Fair, the visual excitement in creating with it hadn't occurred to me: picture frames, nature scenes, bulletin board borders and book covers are but a few ideas translatable into faith education.

At the same time, it recycles paper which might have become 'waste.') Come to the fair!

The Clergy and Religious Staff in Parishes. Call on these friends of Religious Education for their expertise in parish and buildings history, often with firsthand knowledge of the facts. Seek out your parish archivist for pictures and artifacts which can profoundly impact learning with a valuable sense of living history. Enjoy the children's response to a church walk (a guided tour of all the interior of the building) given by their pastor. Seek out these folks, too, as guest speakers to the children about their religious calling and work in ministry. A valuable resource in our midst!

Friendly, Knowledgeable Folk In The Parish Community. Elicit special expertise and faith formation pointers from those whose occupation or profession can give Christian witness to young people. Doctors, nurses, counselors, mental health workers, musicians, artisans, soup kitchen managers are just a few whose lives might 'speak volumes.' Consider, too, enlivening gospel stories with the presence of farmers, bread bakers, fishermen, a vestment maker or a tax-collector. Christ's words, "I was a stranger and you welcomed Me" resound more profoundly from an immigrant whose story of fleeing persecution is shared with incredulous grade-schoolers. The human resources right in our community's midst can serve to illustrate Christian witnessing and living faith, an impression the creative catechist will not hesitate to encourage in children. We need but to seek out and invite into our classrooms the very people who exemplify the gospel living we wish to present to young people.

Shops and Services In Our Neighborhoods. Be on the alert for products and service available locally which can be sources of supplies or information. For those indispensable supplies needed in activities, become acquainted with art supplies stores, woodworking shops, paper producers, office supply houses, printers, video rental stores, the public library (which often offer films for loaning,) music stores, remnant shops and hardware stores. I once obtained forty miniature loaves of bread from a bakery which makes and uses them for promotional purposes. The children preparing for First Communion that year delighted in taking them home with the direction to "lead a bread-breaking prayer" at a family meal. This catechist was delighted, too, in the enchanting loaves for this purpose. It is often in our going the extra mile that we find that article or person that can help us give our lessons that spark of interest and exciting dimension of creativity.

Once one is into the habit of resource acquisitiveness the creative catechist in us delights in happening upon a particular 'find,' one which will serve well to stimulate young learners. One day in a paint store, I noticed a small, child-sized cardboard boat which was being used for display purposes. Could I, perhaps, have the charming construction when the manager no longer had use for it? A few weeks later, a phone call notified me that the little boat was mine – the perfect aid in teaching several gospel stories in which the craft is featured.

On a grocery shopping errand, I once delighted in seeing a dozen very large, colorful butterflies suspended in the store. Acquisitiveness won out, as, later, I was given the lovely 'creatures' which were dazzling in a classroom's Easter corner.

Educational resources abound, and enticingly await the faith teacher's discovery. What untold possibilities likewise await the creative catechist's utilizing of them in classroom experiences which make faith come alive for children!

RESOURCES THAT CLARIFY

Children called to hear the Good News come to us with various degrees of spiritual awareness and intellectual aptitude. They come with individual learning needs and styles of processing understanding. Some are visual learners, others are audio scholars. Still others learn principally through their kinetic avenues. These learning diversities within the group will call for the utilizing of many resources which will aid the catechist in responding to these differences. Consider having the following teaching aids available as media for conveying the Truth to young minds and hearts in the faith education setting.

Some of the properties might be kept readily available in the room. Others will need to be common to one's program, and stored conveniently. They all will be effective lesson-boosters, especially when a broader measure of understanding is in order. These resources will provide that dimension of comprehension which takes the children beyond the 'word' of the catechist or the textbook, and into the meaningful faith experience sought. "Getting it" and "catching the faith message" is simply more achievable with the use of resources which directly stimulate the child's learning powers. The creative catechist will value such resources for their clarifying results.

A VCR, Video Cassette Tapes and Television. These resources offer the catechist many advantages in education, since today's children are highly 'video-oriented' and usually respond well to this media. Yet, it is well advised that its used be conservative, the less likely would its appeal be 'worn out.' Their value in religious education is evident when children view tapes when content is relative to the given lesson, whose subject matter is pertinent to the children's maturity, and whose message is enriching to the lesson's concept. The creative catechist will choose discriminately the tapes for use, reviewing them with the above criteria in mind, and being guided by the recommendations from other catechists who have show the material. A diocesan resource center's catalog will conveniently list available tapes, their educational merit and recommended age level.

Consider, also, the production of your own taped material for use with certain lessons. I have videotaped a typical Sunday Mass, capturing not only its various highlights, but many of the families preparing for First Communion who would be viewing it for instructional purposes. It provided much delight in seeing "our church," "our pastor," and "ourselves"! Such familiarity sustained keen interest and produced learning as they were shown during lessons on the various parts of the Eucharist liturgy. One might tape a home video of a family's celebration of Sunday or another liturgical highlight, or the natural beauty during the seasons as seen in one's neighborhood, or perhaps of the welcoming of a newborn baby into a family. Surely, these tapes and 'stories' make effective resource tools which belong in catechetics.

Educational Films, Slides and filmstrips As valuable to the faith educator as are videotapes. Their selection criteria is the same as given above for videotapes. This lively medium invariably stimulates children's curiosity and involvement, as it delivers that dimension of pleasurable learning associated with film viewing. Likewise, be advised of films, slides and filmstrips through the education resources offered in your diocese resource center.

A Tape recorder and Audio Tapes. Let the children be greeted with the sound of happy faith music, especially with those recorded by and for children. Cary Landry's "Hi God" cassettes (I, II and III, IV, NLRC) especially fill children's need for upbeat, short and meaningful songs which can quickly become favorites upon repeating.

Are the students learning a particular song, perhaps for a liturgy or a prayer service? Familiarize them with its music and words through hearing them on a tape. Committing it to memory will be so much easier when it's 'sing-along time.' This resource tool 'stars' for more than its musical value. Try recording the youngsters' prayers or stories for their listening and learning pleasure. (I have come to consider the ready tape in a recorder as equal to film in a camera, for the variety of captivating subjects it can capture in one's classroom!)

Likewise, record yourself reading a gospel story, or any appropriate story or poem to enhance a lesson. This attention getter will amaze everyone! Play the story as it works into the lesson, perhaps accompanied with simple hand puppets or pictures. Enjoy commercially-made tapes of Bible stories while showing it unfolding in an accompanying picture book or on the flannelgraph. Children of all ages enjoy cassettes of Nature sounds, such as flowing water, thunder, rain or blowing wind. These are strongly appealing to the images conjured up in hearing certain favorite gospel stories. The creative catechist will make practical and educational use of tape recorders and audio tapes.

A Camera. Loaded and ready for capturing the children at various occupations during classtime, for the fun of arranging them on a bulletin board. Create a display under the Scripture banner: *I have called you by name – you are mine.* Or place each photo on a bright blue drop of water pouring out of a huge paper shell on a large piece of paper holding the brightly lettered proclamation: *We are baptized. The life of Jesus Risen is growing in our hearts.* Children so enjoy seeing their pictures, and making all the more personal the visual and spiritual message which they have helped to portray. First Communicants delight in their large picture-poster announcing their coming 'big event' to all their parish family who, in seeing the children's pictures, feel more acquainted with them.

Flannel Graph Boards and Pictures – For 'bringing to life' the Bible scenes and stories presented to youngsters. The flockingbacked, colorful figures and scenery are placed on large, flannel-surfaced background drawings, and are moved about as the story unfolds. This media is always a favorite because of the visual reality it evokes, and for the learning power it stimulates when children both see and hear the story happening. Excellent visualizations of Old Testament, New Testament and Life of Jesus stories are published by Standard Publishing of Cincinnati, Ohio and by Scripture Press Publications, Wheaton, Ill. The appeal of Flannel Graph (or Pict-o-graph) resources increases multifold when the children, having delighted in the story as observers, confidently illustrate it for their peers. Flannel Graph stories make the desired lasting impression gratifying to both catechist and students.

Bible Stories and Faith-building Books. Gather plenty of well-illustrated material which relates the Word meaningfully to young spirits. Collect tasteful books which help to draw a moral point or which have faith-inviting themes. Ever interesting to young students are the Arch Books Bible stories which are fascinating in their often poetic narration and colorful caricature drawings. These, published by Concordia Publishing House, St. Louis, Mo., individually tell scores of familiar Bible stories, and together comprise a modestly priced library of favorite narrations. What magic unfolds when children gather attentively to hear these stories, and others, such as *Swimmy* by Leo Leonni (Knoph/Pantheon,) *The Very Hungry Caterpillar* by Eric Carle (Philomen) or *Hope for the Flowers* by Trina Paulus (Paulist Press). What delight young minds and hearts discover in the spiritual 'threads' woven into storybooks by Tommy de Paola. The attentive catechist who is reading stories for faith-building understands that it is complete only when the listener hears the story with the heart, allowing its message to speak, and to confirm its power by realizing it in faith. Such is the potentiality of the child's concentrated listening to the Word in a well-read story.

Puppets. A universally acclaimed teaching tool to accompany and express any drama, story, song and one's own creativity! It's easily the young child's choice of media for creative clarification. Let every catechist acquire a collection of captivating puppets! Have some for Bible-story telling (Jesus, a man, a woman, a child, a rich person, a poor person, a shepherd, a king, etc.). have others on hand with a contemporary personality to help with illustrating present-day situations (adults, children, pets, older people, babies, etc.).

Stick puppets are easily created. For the simplest construction, cut out and mount pictures of characters found in used religion texts or magazines. Apply them to sturdy tagboard, and glue each to a stick for handling. Large, expressive faces, alone, which children have made might become stick puppets, with tongue depressors and ice cream sticks making handy holders for smaller scale figures.

Other adaptable materials for creating puppets are clothes pins, paper sacks, gloves, wooden spoons and socks. Children respond quite readily to the opportunity for designing their own 'character' out of a supply of staples such as construction paper, buttons, trimmings, fabric, wood scraps, plastic eyes, felt scraps, paint and color markers.

Exaggeratedly large stick puppet figures can bring visual reality and delight to faith lessons. For example, try using a huge, sparkly sun and an even larger gray cloud to portray our Christlight being visible and "used" when we say "yes" to loving, and being "covered over" when one chooses to say "No" to loving. (The cloud which has covered the light "goes away" as one is sorry and forgiven!) A sturdy stick is secured to each figure. Another very large puppet useful in the classroom is the covenant sign of the rainbow (with learning possibilities from God's Covenant through Noah in Genesis 9:12-16, to the gift of God's grace – life upon the newly baptized). Try these large-scale rod puppets for effective illustration of the Creation Story: stars, sun, moon, animals, plants and people.

Hand puppets (those which are 'worn' and have some head and arm movement) are practically constructed from small pieces of felt or sturdy cloth, with the front and back sewn together, allowing for the neck opening. Use a Styrofoam ball, preferably one which is egg-shaped and slightly carved out for one's finger placement. Attach facial features cut from fabric or paper scraps. Add fake fur for men's beards. A shawl or wraparound head covering gives further character and security of manipulating the puppet. If the hand puppet is made of two pieces of fabric which includes the head, add the facial features, hair or covering after stuffing the head lightly with cotton.

The creative catechist (who enjoys a pun) might "try one's hand" at making puppets out of papier-mâché. These usually become fascinating molded heads, and sometimes expressive hands, completed with costumes of cloth. Talk about supremely individual expressive possibilities! How satisfying to create and paint and make a story come alive with such a media.

A very large, sturdy box, cut with a viewing hole, will make a plausible puppet theater, especially with drawings and other attractive embellishments, such as curtains for added charm.

Add to your resource library some of the illustrated handbooks for puppet creation and their usefulness found at Christian education centers and craft shops. One which especially appeals to early childhood educators is *Easy-To-Make Puppets And How To Use Them* by Fran Rottman (Regal Books Division, G/L Publications, Ventura, CA, 1980).

A Pictures File. Obtained from religious supply stores and gleaned from magazines, used religion texts and calendars, pictures do speak volumes! Keep them large, colorful, mounted onto sturdy paper, and, if possible, stored according to themes. Pictures bring lessons to life, provide valuable identification and reflection for children. A bulletin board studded with colorful pictures around a theme or scripture verse is pure attention-getting magic in the faith classroom. Pictures confirm Truth for children when they reflect the value being learned. Look for Bible story sets of illustrations such as those produced by David C. Cook Pub., drawn by Richard and Frances Hook: these are sensitive portrayals of the life of Jesus, the Parables, the Miracles and Early Christian Life. Other favorite sets of pictures are the *"12 Jesus Pictures" Bible Pictures and Present Day Pictures* offered by Standard Publishing Co., Cincinnati, Oh.

Children-made Musical Rhythm Instruments. Simple, childcrafted rhythm devices become a rewarding resource for those times when musical expression is 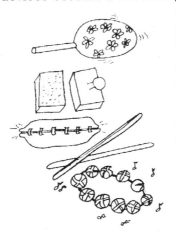 on the agenda. Children enjoy and respond to songs and their catchy rhythms. Help them to make simple 'shakers,' tambourines, straps of bells, rhythm sticks, sandpaper blocks and chiming triangles to keep time to the songs as they enjoy them. Children's craft books detail well the materials needed, their construction, and suggestions for decorating the creations. Let the catechist's and students' ingenuity abound in using cast off items, such as paper towel dowels (put several small stones inside and close off both ends with wrapping paper held fast with rubberbands,) elastic 'jingles' (stitch various-sized bells to strips of elastic, sized to wrists and/or ankles. To make 'shakers,' sew Styrofoam or paper bowls placed face-to-face, with small stones popped inside before closing. Be inventive with the bits and pieces of materials and containers you and the children can gather. No persuasion to "shake, rattle and roll" will be needed the next time you start the music, or songs need some singing!

A Gospel Story "Dress Up" and Props Box. For the children's dramatic portrayals of Biblical scenes and events, which unfailingly elevate and enliven both their participation and learning powers. Have available some costume materials, such as large pieces of rather coarse fabric (for robes,) smaller folds of colorful squares (for head covers,) and lengths of cording for holding it all together around the waist. Discarded bathrobes become garments. When free to create dramatic costumes, children thrill in their innovations and delight in the transformation which they make possible. The story becomes so much *more* right before their eyes! Learning opportunities open up in their imaginative role-playings. Meaning and sense enter into the spirit as characters are personified. All are, when we provide for them, but possibilities in a box.

Certain "Gospel Props" are a "must" for rounding out creative dramatics with youngsters. Seek out suggestions for available items when reading over the story in preparation time. Some storable articles will include a cane or crutch, a soft stuffed lamb, a traveling (drawstring) bag, play money, palm-sized stones, a fish-net, a scroll, seeds, some yeast, pearls, a jar of oil, a lamp, a towel and at least one large water jug.

Other gospel props which can be made available at the time of their use include a bowl of water, a basket of five loaves and two dried fish, a plate of flat (Eastern) bread and cup of wine (apple juice suffices well). The more realistic we can help children make the dramatic moments, that much more will the story's impact be upon them. Tables, chairs, benches and small pieces of carpet can become set props, adding to the realism.

An invaluable catechetical resource for developing creative drama for education and worship is found in the handbook *Acting Out the Miracles and Parables* by Sr. Mary Kathleen Glavich, SND, (Twenty-Third Publications). Her work includes 52 five-minute plays on the Lord's miracles and parables, as well as a selected bibliography to assist the catechist with background understanding. Seek out other guide books, too, for dramatic play production. Such books in your resource library will help to generate interest and, above all, learning in faith lessons. Simple costumes, props and settings, when used in children's "acting out" the stories encountered in Scripture, help them immeasurably to establish the story's setting, to validate its words and actions and – most critically – to enter into its meaning in a qualitative way. They are teaching resources supreme!

"NATURAL" RESOURCES: GIFTS OF NATURE

The 'wonder' to the acquisitive catechist is that so many of the applicable resources for our lessons are available close at hand; many are literally free and simply waiting to be employed. Fine-tuning our sense of discovery we can, for example, find materials in the natural world which can be gathered, collected and used actively or passively in our faith teaching. The creative catechist might choose to set up a Wonder Table in the classroom, filling it with gleanings from forest, shore and garden. The interesting items can become part of the faith environment we create. The intriguing display will arouse curiosity with its "please touch" sign and a handy, large magnifying glass for close-up inspections. With little encouragement, the students, too, will delight in adding their 'finds' to the Wonder Table. The gleanings become an arresting focus for sensory hungry children as they enter the room, and during their periodic free moments.

Nature's gift might, indeed, be put to work actively in our lessons as visual aids. A lush ivy or bean plant readily illustrates the vine of Christian life of John 15. The eyes of faith teach the young soul what words alone cannot convey. Rocks, large and solid, help children to visualize and interiorize the everlasting strength of the Lord. ("The Lord is my Rock, my refuge in whom I trust" from Psalm 18 printed in a small sign near the rock becomes a living word for the viewers). Other discoveries might be utilized in a lesson's creative activities such as in sand castings, in a seasonal montage or collage of Autumn praise creations. The ideas and possibilities for using Nature's treasures in faith education are, indeed, as numerous as the items themselves awaiting our discovery and creative ingenuity.

Include these ideas in your Natural Resources collection and enjoy their exciting possibilities. And "Happy Gleaning"!

Seeds of All Kinds, Sizes and Shapes. (Is there ever a greater mystery in our midst than the lowly *seed*? What infinite spiritual connotations can be made from pondering a seed!) Collect numerous familiar plant seeds, glue a few examples of each kind onto an attractive board, label them, and hang the display at eye evel. Enjoy their variety in shapes, textures and sizes. Ponder prayerfully the mystery of life secured within each one, the power of water upon the dry husk, and Christ's words, "Unless a seed falls into the ground," as well as other parables citing the power within seed. Wonder together what the seed needs to allow to happen in order for *life* to become. What if it is unwilling? afraid? Content to be as it is? Are we ever like the seed? Compare the life-implosion to our own Baptismal life. To what will the growth lead? Might the seed of our faith be looked upon as tenderly as God regards the tiny seed in our hand?

Have the children save and bring in dozens of easily obtainable seeds which they encounter, such as watermelon, pumpkin and apple seeds. Glue the dry seeds into the shape of a rosary on a firm cardboard. Once dried in place, the 'rosary' mysteries can be labeled, the 'beads' prayers indicated. What a meaningful, creative way to celebrate October, the Month of the Holy Rosary!

Continue the reference to abundant life from the seed by discussing the Creator's generosity (why not one seed inside a pumpkin? Why so many?). Talk of

God's creativity (what is God revealing by such a mysterious way of making life?). Praise God for variety (which might God be showing about His power and ability?). Youngsters enjoy pondering such mysteries, and consequently reveal to us who listen "between the words" the astounding depth of their spirituality thanks to the absorbing enigma of the seed.

As a vehicle into prayer, the lowly seed serves well. Have each child select a seed out of a variety offered. With soft, instrumental music in the background, ask them to hold their small seed in the palm of their hand. Offer no words, only stillness. Let the child get to 'know' his seed, talk to it in his heart, ask it questions, wonder what it could become; in other words, *love* his little seed. Ask them to look at the seed as God does. What does God see inside each seed? Let intuition and spiritual sensitivity draw the child deeply into its message and mystery.

Of course, the planting of seeds should be a priority activity for children, for the purpose of following through "the promise" within the seed. Dish gardens made in aluminum foil pie plates are simple and successful possibilities. After planting tiny 'crops' such as radishes, wheat, grass, marigolds or impatiens, they will enjoy arranging small interesting rocks, sticks or animal figurines within their garden. What creativity can spring forth what delight and indeed, what *faith*!

Leaves, Pods and Dried Grains. Especially in the Autumn, these gifts of the earth are lovely evidence of harvest, seasonal rhythms and God's provision. Gather them, cluster them in a display, decorate with them and pray with them. Children holding colorful leaves while in a prayer circle find praise is a 'natural' response. Golden wheat and other grains easily bring to mind the heartiness of the bread they will let themselves "become." A display of some wheat and bread will help children preparing for Eucharist to readily connect the fullness of life which is potential in the grain. Add a sign near these, along with some wheat grains and some ground flour, imprinted: "Little slice of bread, what were you before you were a little slice of bread?"

Inevitably, children, guided by our observation, will come to appreciate that within the fruit of a plant is stored seed for more new life. Help them see this mystery at work in their own lives as they open the wheat head or a fat pod to reveal the waiting seeds, that in the works of love which they do (which are signs of the fruit of the Holy Spirit within them) are seeds of other impulses to act with love. What we do reverberates and echoes into other lives like 'love seeds' ready to sprout with life. So much "theology" hides within these natural resources! Children are intuitively responsive to our revealing it if we would but tap into its richness for them.

Plants, Sprouting Bulbs and Vines. Set out a veritable minigarden of healthy vegetation in children's faith learning environment. Their value is both visual enjoyment, and, of course, "scientific," yet each is illustrative of the gift of life as well as the power of their scriptural references. Might plants seem so like ourselves! Thriving in 'good soil' of faith, responsive to regular waterings of the sacrament's renewal, reaching inevitably for the light of Christ these are but a few spiritual comparisons which can be drawn for their learning. Is someone growing sluggishly, or even witheringly? What happens when the 'fertilizer' of prayer is applied? Studying close up the growth of simple Morning Glory or Scarlet Runner Bean plants easily discloses the necessarily connected life of the Vine and the Branches of John 15's compelling image.

In the burying of tulip or crocus bulbs deep into rich, dark earth, the child is able to express the mystery of dying, of hope and faith, and ultimately of the joy which the sight of shoot and flower reflect of resurrection. Making bulb planting a Lenten prayer activity will offer children a valuable sensory experience unlike any other to help them understand the mystery of Christ's dying and rising up to new life. The very action of planting, literally burying, the bulb, followed by its seeming 'death' draws the child into a deeper plane of thinking – that of believing. "What is faith," then, we can ponder with them. Is it not willingness to let God 'work' as He wills for the bulb and in our lives? How, too, is Christ's risen life different, from His prior earthly life as the rising plant is also different, 'new,' indeed it is the very glory of the bulb! Do we see in risen life (in the flower, in Christ, and in our life) the *more* which God continually promotes?

The planting of bulbs can easily demonstrate, during the Lenten season of renewal, the child's own 'burying' of unloving habits – willingly 'dying' to them – and one's hope for 'higher' ways of living from resolution made in the light of the Paschal Mysteries celebrated. How effectively the creative catechist can draw upon plants for their correlation to spiritual life for the children's benefit.

A Butterfly Cocoon. Keep this highly mysterious "secret," attached to its branch, in a strategic location for observation and fascination. Have pictures and books detailing the changes which are hidden, but happening to the pupa. Is not the chrysalis similar to the husk of the plant bulb? How tremendously God can work in ways unseen to our eyes! Watch together as just prior to releasing its 'new life' the chrysalis becomes transparent, revealing its interior beauty: wings, ready to unfold. What delight God takes in our 'interior' changes! How God glories in our new life, each time we respond to grace and in our ultimate new life of resurrection! Fruitful discussion for the sake of spiritual correlation can be helpful when children tell of the limitations of the lowly caterpillar, how curtailing its life is in this form. What of our interior life before the gift of salvation and grace? What, then, of the expansion of life when Christ entered and we were changed, 'lifted up,' 'given wings' at our Baptism? Talk of the butterfly being the glory life of the caterpillar – after it entered its 'death' in the cocoon. Rejoice in prayer over how much God delights in giving us unlimited possibilities just as the new butterfly seems to now enjoy.

Gifts of the Sea. Collect and arrange an intriguing display (upon a small 'shore' of beach sand).of all kinds and sizes of shells, stones and driftwood. Help the children to value their intricate designs, colors, shapes and patterns. Here, again, are prayer-activity possibilities. Does a particular shell remind me of myself in any way? What of the Creator's power do we detect in the shell? Who 'hears' the ocean's sound in the large conch shell? Tell of the beauty and design in the items which, in reality, are castoffs and discards. Let the children reflect quietly while holding a shell and listening to an audiotape of sea and shore sounds. Wonder together why Jesus chose to spend so many hours at the lakeshore. What have we found refreshing in being there, too? Shells and driftwood fascinate children and are ideal hands-on materials for leading the heart into the Creator.

Sheepskin and Some Raw Wool. For the value of touching and seeing the 'real thing' when a Bible story refers to the shepherd and sheep, little will substitute for the learning through these senses. Feeling lanolin-rich, curly fleece impacts the Scripture reference with a gentle force. Handling the tough, weatherproof hide verifies its use as a sturdy clothing for a shepherd. Offer tactile opportunities by setting out these on the Wonder table. Add a card bearing a sheep or shepherd reference such as John 10:1-8 or Psalm 23 where protection and care are inferred in the words.

An Abandoned Bird's Nest. Another fascinating 'find' for the Wonder table in any season. Add a few feathers, tiny clay eggs and a small, realistic bird found in a craft supply store. Enjoy discussing the God-given instinct which birds employ so successfully. What rewards do we have when we 'obey our instincts'? Marvel together at the craftiness shown from the ingredients used in the nest's construction. Because birds are voices of God in their own right, appreciate anew the joy which their songs bring to us. Can we identify a few familiar calls? This resource is a singular example of God's provision for His beloved creatures. Be refreshed in exploring it.

A Bowl of Water. The primary 'sign of life' in both our natural world and that of our spirit realm through Baptism. Its ordinariness might diminish our profound wonder at its power to provide so essentially for life. Together recapture the utter sense of water as the gift it is. Provide reflective opportunities to drink it, pour it, bathe the hands slowly in it, refresh plants with it and wipe a surface clean with it. Count the ways water is used in but one day in one's life. Demonstrate its use in Baptism. Discuss the kind of "life" which begins with the pouring of water at Baptism. What might be symbolically cleansed in one's spirit? Recount our custom of signing ourselves with some holy water upon entering the church. What are we remembering? Gather some rainwater in a dish to bring to prayer of thanksgiving. Capture the power of water to 'magnify' when we see through it, to 'make more' of a substance (such as a dry sponge) when we soak in it. Be in awe of water's power and motion in a strong current. Do we find some spiritual correlation to these forces as we think on the life we are called to live in the power of our Baptism? Are we not called to 'magnify' the presence of God, to 'make more' love in our world through God's grace? Are we to be part of a motion, or momentum, or the flow of the revelation of God in our families?

Let children return often to the mystery and profundity of water, for they will allow it to slake their 'thirst' for the Truth it reveals.

A Basket of Fruit. Here, too, is a natural resource with great sensory appeal and many possibilities for spiritual correlation. Children will readily recognize beauty, variety and God's provision in their pondering of an appealing cluster of fruits. Lead them into wonder at the Creator's delight in designing so many shapes, tastes, colors and sizes. Provide enough for each child to select a fruit to hold and consider, looking at it as God must do, valuing its uniqueness. Allow for the enjoyment in eating some of their choice, comparing tastes, sharing discoveries and observations. Which must be peeled? How are the seeds confined?

Use a collection of fruit to reflect upon the Gifts of the Spirit accounted in Galatians 5:22-24. Teach them of the singularity of each of the 'fruits' of the Spirit. Each has a distinct 'flavor,' power and way of being manifest within people. Yet all are of the one Spirit and are offered to show forth God's life in us. Value together the goodness of God in promoting such a 'harvest' of good within our lives. After naming the Fruits of the Spirit (love, joy, peace, patience, kindness, goodness, faithfullness, humility and self-control) let the students print them on little cards. With the aid of a toothpick taped to the back of each, poke the namecard into one of the fruits in the basket for further visual impact. The familiar reference to the name will easily be retained.

Consider surprising the students with the questions, "What does God hide in an apple? After they have given several obvious answers (juice, seeds, pulp, etc.) cut the apple, very ceremoniously, on its equator. Ask one of the children to separate the two halves, then show the surprise answer. There, to be enjoyed and awed by all, is a star!

A Moss-Covered Rock. Displayed on the classroom's *"Life"* table, this velvety, green object will visually stimulate and tactilely thrill youngsters who are growing in appreciation and wonder of the gift of life. Likely to be found in a moist garden or forest in the spring, a mossy rock perfectly illustrates (1) the utter "compulsion" of God to create life ("God can't stand for there *not* to be life!," claims an 8-year-old,) (2) the promise of God to give life wherever there is reception to it, and (3) the power within life which causes it to cling and grow and become! With a magnifying glass handy, explore the intricate plants on the rock, marveling at their beauty and completeness. Ponder the solidarity in appearance as, together the tiny plants create a 'community.' Are these not the very signs of the Body of Christ, dependent upon our Rock: each of us a unique, complete creation, together one beautiful unit?

Enjoy occasionally spraying the mossy rock with life-giving water. What can we believe is "in" the water for the moss, as it is for us in the life-giving sacraments of Christ? Enjoy praying Psalm 144, which this resource quite easily prompts. A simple object, the mossy rock offers profound visual connection to the Truths being interiorized.

A Bouquet of Flowers. Besides being a visual joy for all, a colorful, seasonal arrangement of flowers gives expression to God's power in creating seemingly endless varieties of shapes, fragrances, sizes and kinds of beauty. Whether enhancing a prayer-corner or Wonder Table, or cheerily greeting arrivals, a bouquet will silently reflect creation's beauty, and will lead children's hearts to wonder in God's lavish artistry. Clever arrangements, such as one in a small, hollowed log or tiny basket, might be formed with autumn leaves, wild grasses and vines added among the flowers. A suggestive sheaf of wheat prominently displayed with flowers in a First Communion classroom will enhance the meaning and impact of this symbol of our Bread of Life.

RESOURCES FROM SCAVENGER-HEAVEN

If ever a definition was apt as a mark of a creative catechist, it is that which the dictionary gives for 'scavenging.' Here is our middle name! To "scavenge," "to salvage usable goods by rummaging through discards." Raise your hand, folks, if you see yourself in these golden words! We are not only an ecologist's dream, we are, with a little practice, developing 'saving' into a full-blown talent. There simply is nothing like a good rummage!

The tricky word in the definition, however, is "salvage," to "save." Alas, although we are dedicated scavengers, we are not *hoarders*. We save things with the practical eye of one who envisions their use and application to creative religious education. We imagine the discard's ability to help create spiritual realization for the child. Creative catechist 'pack rats,' therefore, have a highly noble purpose in scavenging. When appears to non-savers as a basement full of junk is, to our rescuing heart, literally boxes and stacks of ideas and possibilities!

Those items formerly destined for the rubbish heap or recycling bin can, indeed, have an important role in our faith teaching work. Most of them are familiar, household items. Most can readily be salvaged by fellow catechists, should there be a particular need for a great number of the items. (Do true salvagers share an unspoken, sympathetic bond?) So, the seasoned scavenger will ask the searching questions when eyeing a 'find,' an educational possibility: "How might I use this in the classroom to build up our faith environment?" and "How could this be turned into an activity which could help children to open up to a Truth?" Perhaps immediate inspiration will offer an answer. Possibly the idea will simmer awhile on imagination's 'back burner.' But, happy are we who save, for we will know where to turn for resources when ideas do start 'cooking'! Creative catechist, think thrice of the potentiality of these discards, of their possibilities in your space and in your lesson.

ICE CREAM BAR STICKS make great holders for small paper or fabric puppets. (Ideal supports for the top and bottom of minibanners.) Use them for finger painting daubers, or for paint stirrers. They're also perfect for making colorful God's Eyes (form a cross with two sticks, wrap colorful yarn around and around, beginning at the center, weaving tightly, and securing the ends. Add a loop for hanging.)

STYROFOAM MEAT TRAYS AND SECTIONED PLASTIC DINNER TRAYS serve as handy holders for paint, scraps or other small items used in crafts, such as beans, shells or alphabet noodles.

SMALL CUBIC BOXES are ideal for an Advent in the home activity such as the following: Select four boxes which have tuck-in lids and which are cube shaped, with each side measuring six to eight inches square. The four boxes will provide 24 sides, or surfaces, one for each day in December, before Christmas. Using those old Christmas cards (scavengers, pat yourself on the back here). Glue one card (cut down to fit the surface) picture to each of the sides of all four boxes. On one corner of the side print the number indicating the day of the month, from 1 to 24. On another corner of the side, print the Biblical citation appropriate for the day, perhaps of the Gospel. When all four boxes have been completed, stack them in an appropriate place for use in family prayer during Advent. The correct date should appear at the top of the 'stack' each day for reference. The day's Gospel is read and insights are shared. Everyone will enjoy the sight of the stack being continually rearranged as the correct date is searched for, especially if the dates are scattered throughout the various sides of the four boxes. The colorful stack provides an inspirational focus throughout the season, as well as a meaningful reference to the richness of its liturgical scriptures.

MEDIUM AND LARGE-SIZED CARDBOARD BOXES are wonderful for building a small-scale Bible-times house in which Gospel scenes will be portrayed,

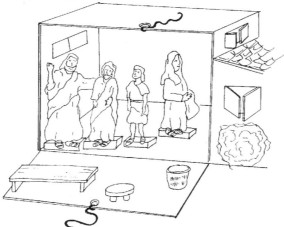

or for constructing a model of the children's parish church. Be choosy about selecting boxes for these projects. When set on its side, the box should be clean, sturdy and with little or no printing visible. Try gluing two or three boxes together to make rooms, using the flaps on them for a portico or other outdoor areas attached to the structure. Cut out doors and windows to lend a realistic look. Flowers cut from a magazine or catalogue and glued on the outside add exciting reality, too.

Use smaller cardboard boxes or shoeboxes to create charming dioramas for depicting the Gospel events being studied. A note on creating with boxes: in our model of our parish church made of both large and small boxes, we were able to portray the important-to-children small rooms adjacent to the church interior by situating small boxes within the larger structure. Thus, a sacristy, music room, vestibule and Reconciliation room were efficiently included in the construction, and gave added pleasure in the children's use of it.

PAPIER-MÂCHÉ FRUIT TRAYS. These easily become a primary child's hanging for sharing and displaying in the home. When the tray is turned upside-down, a simple design such as a Christian symbol or single word is penciled on the back. This design is made up of dots, spaced about ½ inch apart. A few design suggestions: Mary's beautiful Advent word *Yes,* the words *Jesus, Spirit, Father* or the child's own name, the child's Baptism date, the familiar symbols of the candle, flame, drop of water, peace sign, star, open Bible, heart and dove. Using a small nail, the child perforates the design dots. With a strip of yarn attached to the top of the tray, it is ready to be hung in a window, the better to allow light to illuminate its inspiring design.

DISCARDED WALLPAPER BOOKS. These hold, literally, pages of possibilities! Use them to cover the interior walls and floors of a model house or church. Some pages might be pebbly or wooden in texture, making them suitable for covering outsides of buildings or for courtyards and floors. Such realism truly enchants children!

Wallpaper sheets make strong covers for child-crafted prayerbooks. Use pages, also, for creating an interesting background on a bulletin board, or for mounting special artwork. Richly-colored or textured pages make attractive lettering or other cut-out shapes for banners or posters.

LIGHTWEIGHT CARDBOARD PIECES (usually found in shirt-packing, and white in color). These are useful for mini-posters, notebook covers, signs and for matting special artwork. Watch children turn them into an attractive hanging by outlining a favorite symbol on one of these cards and, with colorful yarn, embroider the symbol with a running stitch along the outline. (Because this activity requires the child to use a fat, craft needle, outline some safety procedures before they launch into their 'sewing'). Complete the activity by threading yarn at the top of the figure, for hanging. Various dried materials, such as beans and rice, can be glued onto the cardboard symbol for added interest after the stitching has been completed.

FROM BOXES TO "HOUSES AROUND OUR PARISH CHURCH" (small to medium sized boxes with lids (6" to 8" inch cube-sized or infant's shoeboxes) are ideal for making children's houses surrounding a larger box in the center replicating the parish church. The sides of each child's box are wrapped around with colored artpaper. The details of doors, windows, flowers, and house number are drawn on. Add the family name, too. With a sturdy, folder folder-roof perched atop each, the houses can be set on a large sheet of paper holding the parish church box in its center. The children will enjoy adding streets, signs and perhaps small toy vehicles to create a model of their parish neighborhood. This simple use of little boxes offers powerful visual impact for the children in seeing their own home as an important part of the whole parish community.

SCRAPS OF YARN, RIBBON, BURLAP, FELT, FABRIC, ETC. These are useful for banners, bulletin boards, and a bazillion art activities. Save, also, ends of sewing trims, buttons and fringes for dressing puppets and decorating other artworks with a 3-D flair.

SMALL CARPET SQUARES OR ENDS OF CARPETING. For story time to sit upon, or prayer time kneel upon.

STURDY TUBINGS FROM PAPER TOWELS AND OTHER SUCH ROLLS. These make great holders for primary children's puppets, with the figure's head set securely on the top. Or tape two short tubes side by side to create a 'set of binoculars' the better to see God's beautiful world. Wrap these in construction paper holding creative designs of thanks for one's gift of sight. Another use: insert one long tube into another which is just a little larger, creating a telescope for peering carefully at Creation. How much more keenly will the young child see the world with new appreciation when viewing it through his lavishly decorated scene-a-scope!

Paint, or otherwise color, short tubes to which bright lengths of yarn or ribbon are tied through punched holes all around the tube. When a length of yarn is added for hanging, and the tube is wrapped in very colorful paper, these become "wind-catchers." Hang them outdoors on bushes and trees to mark a celebration of Pentecost.

USED, DRIED COFFEE GROUNDS. Use these to create 'roads,' 'paths,' or 'gardens' when pictures call for an added dimension and realism. Spread a layer where needed, over brushed-on glue, shake off excess, and let the stunning effect dry. (One third grader used coffee grounds for his pictures of apostles' beards, which turned out to be a clever touch!)

BABY FOOD JARS are handy for holding individual amounts of paint, or for filling with water when study calls for children's individual appreciation of the element, perhaps in prayer, when eye-to-heart contact with Baptism's blessing is desired. Use these resources for storing small supplies, or for childrens' collections of seeds.

PLASTIC "SQUEEZE" CONDIMENT OR HONEY BOTTLES can be used for holding you own home-made glitter glue! Mix water-based glue with glitter, 50% each, there you have countless ways for children to decorate their artwork.

USED GREETING CARDS AND CHRISTMAS CARDS. Cut out small bits of scenery from the cards, mount them on a piece of Styrofoam or wood. Add helping props such as moss, dried coffee grounds for soil, and create a garden or stable scene which can hold a special place on the child's prayer table, or be given as a gift. (When the wood or foam block holding the scene, tiny animals, too, can be added to it.)

MAGAZINES AND OLD CALENDARS are useful for their wonderful picture value in projects such as a montage or collage and especially in their possibilities as teaching aids. Can one ever have enough good pictures?

In short, dear fellow scavenger, when considering any discard's ultimate value, just remember the creative catechist's motto: *When in doubt, save it!*

CATECHIST-CREATED RESOURCES

Some of the most effective resources to be enlisted in religious education are those which can be created by the catechist. These home-made products can contribute immeasurably to children's interest and learning stimulation. As is true for all good resources, these, too, can often make the difference between unproductive boredom and sustained participation in our classes.

Out of our compassion for the faith-hungry child, let us provide a visual diet of captivating, spiritually nourishing aids to learning. Let these original, sometimes humble, supports serve to arouse children's curiosity and energize their impressionable minds. Does a particular concept in your lesson need simplifying? Explaining? Visualizing? Will concretizing a gospel Truth help youngsters to interiorize it? By being supportive with graphic educational assistance, we, as catechist, are sincerely expressing our deep commitment to their lasting learning. In our willingness to respond to such a call to creativity, and ready to enjoy its rewards, we will find the unique satisfaction in meeting a deep-seated need of the child's spirit.

What will such resource-creating require of us? Realistically, it will depend upon how much time, energy and ingenuity we will want to invest in them. Further, consideration needs to be given to the storage of the resources. Those which are durably and sturdily made will last over much use in a clean, dry place and when not in use. It may be feasible to get together with another, or several other, catechists to pool inventiveness, materials, and enthusiasm. Yet, let it be emphasized, that you will find a special joy in exercising your particular ingenuity in creating resources. Indeed, I have often felt a kind of birthing experience in turning out an interesting visual aid, and an accompanying excitement in later sharing it with children. I believe that this process exemplifies so well our call to "give of the gift which you have received."

Consider creating the following resources to enliven learning and for holding the attention of young learners.

A LARGER-THAN-LIFE FELT ROSARY BOARD. On a 40-inch square of sturdy posterboard, form a rosary made of 1½ inch felt circles glued in place. Plan

for each decade to be shown in a different, bright color, with the "Our Father" beads in a singular color of their own. An arrow imprinted with the guide words "I believe . . ." is placed near the crucifix to indicate the Apostles Creed prayer. Identify with an arrow the "Our Father" and the first "Hail Mary" beads at the beginning of each decade as well. Likewise, arrows indicating the place for the "Glory be . . ." prayer are also glued in the appropriate places. Place on the board printed copies of each of the rosary's prayers, as well as the names of the 15 mysteries of the rosary, accompanying them with pictures of their meditation event. Use the colorful board to teach the rosary, particularly during the months of May (the month honoring Mary) and October (the month of the holy rosary).

AN "OUR LIFE IN JESUS" JAR aids in intuiting how completely is our union with Jesus. Fill a large (approx. 40 oz.) glass jar with water. Cut out the shape of a person from a 5" by 8" sponge. Submerge the figure in the water, helping it stay below the surface by squeezing out the air bubbles. Close the jar lid tightly. Here comes the fun of this resource. Ask the children what they see here. Most will answer that "the sponge is in the water." Though it is true, ask them to see more. (Be patient, now, to increase their joy in revelation.) They will eventually say that "the water is in the sponge"! Let this really soak in! One is in the other! When asked what they think this has to do with ourselves and Jesus, their wonderings will lead them to reveal that we are in Jesus because of our Baptism, (as seen by the sponge in the water) and that Jesus is in us (the water in the sponge) and, that emphatically, the two are inseparable. In prayer with this resource, let there be time for their enjoying just thinking about this Truth, so profound, yet so simple.

A PAIR OF MIRRORS THAT TEACH. Mount two mirrors, one a standard type, one a magnified type, side by side onto a large posterboard or heavy cardboard. Give them an attractive, bright background. Invite children to flash their beautiful "child of God" smiles, and to think about the magnifying which God's does within us through grace. What gifts and personality traits are enlarged for God kingdom purposes? Think how much God loves to make our lives "more," really magnified! Print colorfully a few apt Scripture verses which add to this resource's impact: "I have called you by name; you are mine" from Isaiah 43:1. "The true children of God are those who let God's Spirit lead them" (Romans 8:14).

A MOBILE OF THE SEVEN SACRAMENTS. Suspend colorful, moving symbols of the sacraments from a coat hanger or wooden rod.

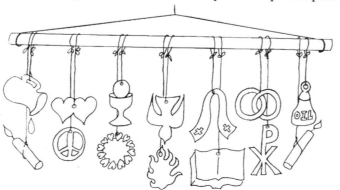

Trace each design from its pattern, or simply enlarge those found in texts. Using sturdy poster-weight paper, cut out the figure, attach threads and hang the symbols at various levels on the hanger. With creativity unlimited, try designing each sign in three-dimensional form, allowing the given design to have its own twirling parts. When hung in a place where the mobile can turn freely, it becomes a bright and exciting learning focus. Suggested sacrament symbols for this resource:

Baptism – pitcher or shell pouring water, candle, jar of oil, robe.

Confirmation – descending white dove, bright flame, gifts of the Spirit.

Eucharist – bread, grapes, wheat, wine in cup, a circle of hearts.

Reconciliation – crossed keys, peace sign, two hearts interlocked.

Holy Orders – a fringed stole with Christian symbols on its ends, open Bible

Matrimony – two gold rings superimposed on the Chi-rho (the Christ-symbol).

The Anointing of the Sick – a jar of holy oil, candle lighted.

GAMES THAT HELP TEACH. Mounted on large, sturdy sheets of cardboard, many games can be created to promote both learning and delight. A large spinning arrow can be affixed to the center of the game board for the taking of turns in a group. Using a strong board for a game allows it to be set upright against a blackboard. Others can be used on desktops or tables, or on the floor. Make the games colorful and appealing with pictures and decorative borders. Try these games, and create others of subjects being studied, and anticipate lots of learning with their use:

How Many Stories About Jesus Can You Tell? Glue to the board a large circle of pictures depicting scenes in Jesus' life. Accompany each with its biblical citation. The child spins the arrow and tells the 'story' pictured where the arrow points. (A good picture source: textbooks no longer in use.)

Recognizing the Corporal and Spiritual Works of Mercy. Glue a large circle of pictures of the action involved in the works of mercy. Add an arrow to the board's center. The child spinning it identifies a picture, naming the work, and explains the pictured example of it. Using cards bearing the name of the Work, the child can tape or tack up its printed title near the picture he/she has correctly identified.

"Review Time" on a pie-shaped wheel. Print questions to aid in reviewing a unit. Affix the arrow to the board, and let the children discover a new way of reviewing their learnings as they spin it, and answer the questions. Playing 'teacher' by calling on the next spinner is always fun for children in this game, too.

We Know Our Prayers. Arrange a circle of printed prayers which are being learned. The child spinning the arrow in the center of the board game recites the selected prayer, perhaps being asked to "spin again," reciting as many (with reading?) as possible. This game will serve the learners well when individual boards are made, and each child challenges him/herself with the learning of those which are familiar in our inherited treasury of prayers and which are committed to memory in the child's early years.

Gigantic Books. Young children delight in seeing and handling objects which are either uncommonly small or large. As a creative catechist, capitalize on this attribute to promote keen engagement and lasting learning through a resource tool called a "gigantic book." Such a captivating medium is made of large (try 24" by 36" pages) white or colored posterboard sheets for firmness and durability. Binder rings, shoe laces or heavy yarn serve to hold the pages together.

Design an attractive cover, large print the text of a concept or story on the pages, and add supportive pictures. For example, a gigantic book might be entitled "How We Receive the Holy Bread and Wine," giving an outline of one's 'steps' in the Communion procedure at Mass, and with appropriate pictures to support the procedure.

Create a gigantic book for enhancing, explaining and magnifying any catechetical concept being presented: The Sacraments, prayers, all about our parish community, what Jesus says about love, etc. Let one of these resources add an exciting dimension to your classroom, for the child who reads it while sitting alone on the floor, for the small group which gathers to be enriched before the classtime begins, or for the large, whole group studying a given concept. "Seeing" really can lead to "believing" with a gigantic book leading the way.

A Wheel of the Liturgical Year. This visual aid will readily clarify for children the overall cycle of the celebration of the church's liturgical year. Have one available to post, particularly when a new season or holy day is approaching. Such a resource helps to visualize the time-frame of each season as well as the seasonal sequence throughout the church year.

Draw a large wheel on a sheet of white posterboard. Divide the circle into segments, pie-fashion, to indicate the seasons and holy days of the church year.

Beginning with Advent, print the name of each season on its portion, and shade it according to its liturgical color. Within a given section, print any special holy days, such as Ash Wednesday, Holy Thursday and Good Friday during Lent. Marian feasts should also be noted. A guide for dividing the circle can be had from the local diocesan Office of Worship. Add a sturdy arrow in the wheel's center for pointing out the various seasons and holy days. Children enjoy noting "what we are in now," and pointing the arrow accordingly. Children of all ages will benefit from this resource, giving them a clear overview of the liturgical year which we celebrate.

Note: if your wheel is large enough, or is mounted onto a larger board, pictures, correlating the seasons may be added to further enrich learning. This resource idea becomes very helpful to learners when it is adapted to a small, individual-scale size, allowing the children to imprint the sections, color in the season and to have their own wheel for reference in the home.

A Moveable Baptism Celebration Scene. Create the realism of a baptism event with a tabletop scene which can be easily manipulated by children for 'acting out' the occasion. From a clothing store catalogue, cut out pictures of family members and guests dressed for a baptism celebration. Choose figures showing the full length of the person, and in equal scale to each other. Include parents, godparents, young children, grandparents, etc. and an infant. Photograph your own parish priest, and size it to the same scale, too. Show him vested for a Baptism. Mount all the pictures onto lightweight cardboard for strength. Cut out each one and, except for the infant, attached a popsicle stick to the back, allowing for it to extend about 2 inches below the figure's feet. Add a piece of flannel to the front of the mother and father figures, and to the back of the baby to allow for easy attachment and removal of the baby.

Prepare for the infant's Baptism celebration by embedding the stick of each of the figures into a semi-circular arrangement on a 12″ by 14″ by 3″ sheet of Styrofoam. Provide a miniature table for the center of the scene, made by wood graining a small, but to scale, lid from a little gift box (try for one about 3½″ by 2″ in size). Glue on four half-length craft sticks to create legs for the table. The following articles, used at a Baptism, should be placed on the table, which is covered with a small white cloth:

> a bowl of water (made from a large bottle cap, spraypainted gold.
> a small container of holy oil, chrism (made from a tiny bottle).
> a miniature white Baptism robe.
> a tiny Bible (handmade, or from a shop selling miniatures).
> a Baptism candle (a white birthday cake candle, set into clay).

This realistic scene will delight and teach children as they manipulate the figures and create the celebration of the sacrament of Baptism. Keep the scene available on a low table for their use.

A Potted Tree-Branch for the Classroom. Secure a sturdy branch (choose one having many small branches attached) in a large pot filled with a prepared mixture of Plaster of Paris. Keep the branch very straight during the setting-up process. Spraypaint the whole branch white for visual appeal. Keep the potted branch handy for holding any variation of "ornaments," such as liturgical season hangings (The Jesse Tree symbols, Holy Week Easter season depictions, etc.,) Christian symbols, Baptism birthday data for each child, photographs of the children and their families, and pictures of natural season's bounty and beauty. Let the branches come alive with children's artwork, also. Enjoy the unlimited possibilities of a classroom branch for promoting learning.

A Five Senses Treasure Box. What captivating self-discoveries children will enjoy with items in this powerful resource! It should be a ready facility in the primary classroom.

Decorate a large shoebox with bright magazine pictures of eyes, noses, hands, ears and mouths to represent the gifts of our five senses. A large bow for the box lid will announce the contents as gifts of the senses, which God loves to have us enjoy!

Deposit within the box a number of items which exemplify the use of the five senses. The following suggestion will be appealing but get "sense-itive," and add others of your imagination:

> pieces of crisp, colored cellophane paper
> pinecones and shells
> small bells in several sizes
> soap, perfume and spices
> squares of several grades of sandpaper
> a small pocket mirror
> cotton balls
> a ball of clay (wrapped in plastic)
> a piece of sheepskin or fleece

a few rough and smooth small stones
a magnifying glass
several sizes of feathers
a small whistle
a box of raisin (for tasting)
sticks of chewing gum
some peppermint and cinnamon candies
a bracelet of colorful beads of all sizes
a pair of sunglasses

Let your 5-senses treasure box intrigue and teach when it's learning time about the gifts of these wonderful powers to be thankful for.

A "We Celebrate Eucharist" Kit. As a display in the classroom, which the children can visit informally, or as a teaching resource to provide them with a hands-on, close-up familiarity with the sacramentals used in celebrating the Eucharist, these articles will serve the needs well:

a paten, made by spraypainting a deep saucer bright gold or silver
a chalice, preferably a shiny "gold" or of ceramic (readily available in re-
   sale shops)
a small, white table cloth and a wide ribbon appropriately colored for the
   current liturgical season
a glass cruet of water, a small white towel, a saucer
two candle stands with ivory-colored candles
a children's Bible; a notebook for loved ones' names remembered
a deep dish of small, round crackers, a carafe of grape or apple juice
a priest's chasuble, made by cutting a circle six feet in diameter from a
   white sheet. Hem the edge. Cut a T-shaped slit in the center to allow
   for vesting. Use fabric paints to add a large Eucharist symbol such
   as wheat, grapes and the cross to the vestment's front.

Watch the children relish learning about the Eucharist celebration while role playing the movements in the Mass. Guide them, using the articles, through each step and its dialogue. Test their retention by having them prepare, present and offer the gifts, read the Gospel story, sing a praise psalm, respond in posture, receive 'Communion,' all with its appropriate dialogue, prayerfully give thanks, and receive the dismissal blessing. This kit, whether presented in individual parts or as a unit, will prove an influential resource for teaching children of all ages about our Eucharist celebration.

An Enormous Footprint Notice Board. This readily understood symbol for the faith learning classroom, the giant footprint (Jesus'? Ours?) will draw children's attention and become a captivating vehicle for notices and inspiration.

Cut out a *very* large footprint, approximately 40″ long, 24″ wide, of sturdy cardboard. Cover the surface with plastic coated adhesive paper in a plain, light color. Hang the footprint in a prominent place, using twine looped at the top, or tack to a bulletin board.

Use this resource for posting notices of the children's birthdays, approach-

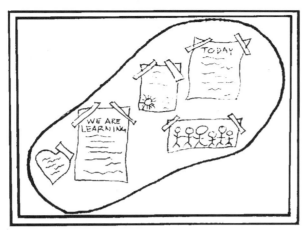

ing church events and holidays, welcome back announcements to absentees, and other messages aimed at youngsters. Inspire them with appropriate. Scripture verses, pictures, goals and learnings taped up or written directly on the footprint with watercolor felt markers. Encourage the children to tape up their own contributions for general notice and see their creativity spring forth.

A Model of the Parish Church. This resource deserves detailed explanation as we consider catechist-created tools for learning. Perhaps you, too, will find that no created resource provides as much enjoyment and learning possibilities as the model of the children's own parish church does for them. I confess that enormous delight has been mine in the creating and using of our model for students of all grade levels. "*Wow!* That's just like *ours!*" has been the delighted chorus upon their discovery of the model church in the classroom.

Begin with a very strong, clean cardboard box which is approximately 30″ long, 18″ wide and 10″ deep. Cut out doors with one side of them left attached for opening and closing. Cut out spaces for windows. On small sheets of clear plastic, paint "stained glass" windows: Glue and frame them into their place. (Cut the church's doors and windows from their appropriate position on the 'real' church structure).

Using corresponding colors, placements and designs likewise related to your own church, complete the exterior and interior of the model. The outside can be covered with art paper, with drawn on lines of wood, brick or stone. By inserting and gluing in place appropriately-sized boxes, small but significant rooms can be set in the interior. Typically, the Reconciliation Room, sacristy, and other areas will be of interest to the children. Folded, medium-weight cardboard can create steps which lead up to the raised level of the church's chancel, the front area where the altar and presider's chair are situated. This area is created higher than the nave by installing an upside-down shallow box in its place, its dimensions being equal to the size of the chancel area.

"Carpet" the floor with soft fabric of appropriate color. (Velour works wonderfully for floor covering.) Paint the uncarpeted floor and interior walls for more reality. Pews can be constructed from lengths of wood, 1″ by 1″ in size, and glued in place. (The exact number of pews isn't a critical matter; positioning the number which will fit camfortable in the model as they appear in the real church is important.)

Take photographs of your church's Stations of the Cross, its religious statues, icons and holy pictures. Mount these on tagboard and place them in their correct areas. Provide the following articles for your model; do not glue them down, so the children can place them appropriately – a tactic helpful both in introducing the model and in reviewing its specifics. Some articles can be found in shops selling furnishings for miniature houses.

A presider's chair
Chairs or benches for altar servers
The Lectern
The Altar, mini-candles for worship
The Tabernacle
Miniature books and Bibles
(placed in the vestibule racks and on
the Lectern)
A Paschal Candle (cut out a picture
of one from a church-supply
catalogue, attach it to a small dowel
with a base)

Tables for the Gifts
and the Priest's chalice
A dish of Altar Breads
(punched holes from an
index card, set into a
tiny clay dish)
A very tiny pitcher of
Wine (really a teeny
bottle of colored water)
A Baptism font, and bowl
of water on it (a bottle,
cap)

Add cut-out photos of your parish priests, altar servers, greeters lectors and ushers. Mount these on posterboard, insert them into a block of wood to keep them upright and movable.

Let your creativity and imagination come into full play in building this delightful resource! Compile suggestions from the children, who will surely sharpen their awareness of the church while it is under construction, and will readily offer suggestions for their model thoughts which will likely occur to them when attending liturgy in their real church.

Top off the creation with a cardboard roof holding a cross in a slit at the top, or one free-standing beside it if your church is so designed. Mount the entire model church onto a sturdy wood board leaving an area around the building for walkways (sprinkle sand on glue-brushed surfaces, paint gray for cement when glue is dry) and shrubbery (crinkle green tissue paper into balls and glue in place against the building, or imbed small, branchy twigs into clay 'trunks' for trees).Teaching, and certainly learning, become pure joy when your model church is the delightful focus.

THE CATECHIST'S FILE OF CREATIVE IDEAS

Perhaps what might be overlooked in a list of suggestions for catechist-created resources is one which is already growing healthy at our fingertips: our own file of suggestions for making lessons come alive, our own ever-expanding, valuable resources. Some ideas may already be tried and true, and in their use we have learned how to make them even more effective. Others are waiting their turn and are full of potential. Building up a useful file of creative ideas for faith teaching should be an ongoing pursuit for the creative catechist who is alert to ways of presenting Truth meaningfully to children.

Make notes of activities, motivators and 'successes' in whatever you have done involving children's faith learning, from classroom lessons to liturgical celebrations. Include a section for family celebrations of faith in the home. Add to your files workshop handouts, patterns, reprints of helpful articles and resource catalogues. Classify suggestions for preparing children for the Sacraments, and those for fostering maturity in the life of grace. Include ideas for prayer, para-liturgies, celebrating Reconciliation and aiding children with special needs. The catechist's file of creative ideas is much like a healthy savings account: it is wealth when you need it.

NEVER UNDERESTIMATE THE VALUE OF A RESOURCE

The committed catechist, convinced of the value of resources in faith education, naturally opens up to the exciting – and seemingly endless – discovery of their possibilities. Resources such as those outlined in this chapter, become for us not an "extra" added on to our central task, not are they seen as just an "enrichment" toward our objectives. *The reservoir of our resources must be considered absolutely essential to the accomplishment of our overall objective,* which is the sprouting and developing of the child's divinely seeded gift of faith! As a creative, resourceful catechist, then, we will continually reach beyond merely stimulating our students. Out of our call to care for the whole learning child, we will strive to meet their various learning needs, to draw forth their budding innate gifts and, above all, to make relevant the very Truths of faith to which our children are disposed. Therein, lies the underlying value of using resources for the catechist! Resources offer *life!* May our use of them give the very drink of life for which children wordlessly thirst. The well is abundant and deep. We have but to lower our buckets.

A. Inspirational reading recommended for the catechist's own development in spirituality

Bodo, Murray, O.F.M. *Jesus a Disciple's Search*. Cincinnati, Ohio: St. Anthony
Messenger Press, 1986. Imprimatur: James Garland, V.G., Archdiocese of
Cincinnati, July 8, 1986.

_____.,*Song of the Sparrow*. Cincinnati, Ohio: St. Anthony Messenger Press,
1976. Imprimatur: Daniel E. Pilarczyk, March 16, 1976.

Cavalletti, Sophia. *The Religious Potential of the Child*. Ramsey, NewJersey:
Paulist Press, 1983.

Donze, Mary Terese, A.S.C.. *Touching a Child's Heart*. Notre Dame, Ind.: Ave
Maria Press, 1985.

Gill, Jean. *Pray As You Can*. Notre Dame, Ind.: Ave
Maria Press, 1989.

Hays, Rev. Edward M. *Prayers for the Domestic Church*.Easton, Kansas:
Shantivanam House of Prayer, 1979.

Hellwig, Monika. *The Meaning of the Sacraments*.Dayton, Ohio:
Pflaum/Standard, 1972.

Kelly, Carole Marie, O.S.F. *Symbols of Inner Truth*.Mahwah, N.J.:
Paulist Press, 1988.

Norris, Gunilla. *Becoming Bread*. New York, N.Y.:
Crown Publishers, 1993.

_____.*Journeying in Place*.
New York, N.Y.: Crown Publishers, 1994.

Puls, Joan, O.S.F. *Every Bush Is Burning*. Mystic, Conn.:
Twenty-Third Publications, 1985.

Rupp, Joyce, O.S.M. *Fresh Bread*. Notre Dame, Ind.: Ave
Maria Press, 1985.

_____.,*May I Have This Dance?* Notre Dame, Ind.: Ave Maria, 1992.
van Breemen, Peter, S.J. *As Bread That is Broken*. Denville, N.J.:
Dimension Books, Inc., 1974. Imprimatur: Joannes
van Deenen, S.J., the Hague, Holland: Sept. 12, 1973.

Wiederkehr, Macrina, O.S.B. *Seasons of Your Heart:*
Reflections and Prayers. Morristown, N.J.: Silver Burdett Co., 1979.

B. Support material to guide the catechist in understanding children's spirituality, and in developing creative activities which support its growth.

Brokamp, Marilyn, O.S.F. *Prayer Times for Primary Grades.*
Cincinnati, Jan. 7, 1987.

Conway, Rev. Thomas D., Frank J. Martino. *Handbook of Creative Activities for Upper-grade Religion Programs.* New York, N.Y.:
William H. Sadlier, Inc., 1972.

DeAngelis, William. *Acting Out the Gospels With Mimes, Puppets and Clowns.*
Mystic, Conn.: Twenty-Third Publications, 1982.

Eroes, Thea. *Handbook of Art Activities for Middle-grade Religion Programs.*
New York, N.Y.
William H. Sadlier, Inc., 1972.

Gamm, Rev. David B. *Child's Play.* Notre Dame, Ind.: Ave
Maria Press, 1978.
Imprimatur: Most Rev. Richard H. Ackerman, S.D., Bishop of Covington.

Glavich, Sr. Mary Kathleen, S.N.D.. *Acting Out the Miracles and Parables.*
Mystic, Conn.:
Twenty-Third Publications, 1988.

Griggs, Patricia. *Creative Activities In Church Education.*
Abingdon/Nashville, Tenn.:
Griggs Educational Service, 1974.

Halpin, Marlene, O.P.. *Puddles of Knowing.* Dubuque, Iowa:
William C. Brown Co., 1984.

Ihli, Sr. Jan, P.B.V.M. *Liturgy of the Word for Children.* New York, N.Y.
Paulist Press, 1979. Imprimatur, Justin Driscoll, Bishop of Fargo,
August 24, 1978.

Manternach, Janaan, Carl F. Pfeifer. *Creative Catechist* Mystic, Conn.:
Twenty-Third Publications, 1983.

Mathson, Patricia. *Burlap and Butterflies.* Notre Dame, Ind.: Ave
Maria Press, 1987.

Reehorst, Jane, B.V.M. *Guided Meditations for Children.* Dubuque, Iowa:
William C. Brown Co. Publishers, 1986.

Rottman, Fran. *Easy-to-Make Puppets and How To Use Them.* Ventura, Ca.:
Regal Books, 1978.